The

Balancing YOUR faith with
GOD'S sovereignty

H. MAURICE LEDNICKY

Printed in
Springfield, Missouri
U.S.A.

Cover Design by Lori Strohmaier

THE DNA OF FAITH
Balancing YOUR Faith with GOD'S Sovereignty

Preface

The questions have been around for a long time. If, as many scholars believe, Job is the oldest manuscript in Scripture, then man has always struggled to know and understand the reasoning of God in relationship to His creation. Job's "friends" concluded that he had done some gross evil or God would not be punishing him in such a harsh manner. Job defended himself and claimed to be innocent of wrongdoing.

And, so the basic question—*Why do the righteous suffer?*—has haunted man's reasoning from the earliest recorded history. In the ensuing years the probe for understanding has expanded significantly.

If God has foreknowledge of all things, then is He the originator of evil, as well as good?

Doesn't God have greater power than Satan? Then why

does He not stop the pain and tragedy that plagues all humans?

Are bad things always the consequence of personal wrongdoing? Is it just that the innocent bear the consequences of the guilty?

Does faith or prayer or a pure, holy heart have any impact of one's circumstances in this life?

In the progressive revelation of God, Christ Jesus came to earth as one among us so we might more fully know God. Today we also have the inspired, written Word of God. While it is true that with such finite understanding none will ever fully comprehend the infinite wisdom of the eternal Sovereign; it is likewise true that the dynamic combination of the <u>Living Word</u> and the <u>Written Word</u> provide spiritual insights to believers today. Nor must one exclude the historical record of millions of saints who make up that *"great cloud of witnesses"* loudly proclaiming God's indisputable faithfulness through every vicissitude of life experienced by man.

During the extended illness and ultimate promotion (to heaven) of our daughter Mischelle, 1 Corinthians 10:13 became a mainstay in my devotional life. *"But remember that the temptations that come into your life are no different from what others experience. And God is faithful. He will keep the temptation from becoming so strong that you can't stand up against it. When you are tempted, he will show you a way out so that you will not give in to it"* (NLT).

Over the past 40 plus years of ministry, traveling across the United States and in more than 50 other nations, I have observed a frightful tendency in many otherwise mature believers. *If there is a breach in faith, it is most likely to come in the area of understanding the scriptural correlation between personal faith and God's sovereign plan.*

Let it be understood that this volume does not attempt to present an antiseptic formula to resolve this dilemma. I do not claim to have some new revelation of eternal truth. What I do have is a lifetime of *experiences*. Experiences of the magnitude and frequency that have forced me to honestly grapple with what biblical faith really means and how it applies to my *here and now*.

Some of what I found in this search was extremely painful. I did not always like what I saw when the Holy Spirit turned the bright, searching spotlight onto my inner heart. While the high purpose of God is always man's redemption, it does not follow that this entails a charmed stroll through life onto the streets of gold. No, in fact, the opposite is true.

Faith will be tested at every turn of the road. Ultimately, it is this *divine process* that slowly but surely shapes a life into the fulfillment of *divine purpose*.

It is important that we establish a foundational premise for our conclusions. Hopefully, we agree on these basic principles as taught in God's Word.

1. There is but **ONE GOD.** He is eternally immutable. As both *creator* and *redeemer* of man, He possesses the

absolute authority in all matters relating to man—both *personal* and *universal.* (Deuteronomy 4:35; Psalm 86:10; Isaiah 43:10; 1 Corinthians 8:4; 1 Timothy 2:5; 1 John 5:7)

2. Through **FAITH** and faith alone, man can have a personal relationship with the Almighty. God's offer for redemption is unilateral—man has nothing with which he can negotiate—and is only received by faith. (John 3:15-18; Romans 5:1,2; Ephesians 2:8,9; Hebrews 11:6)

3. As redeemed children of this sovereign God, it is absolutely imperative that we strive to develop a **CONFIDENT TRUST** that His way is *good, right,* and *perfect* in every circumstance. This is the highest expression of faith one can offer before the God he loves and serves. (Deuteronomy 32:4; Psalm 18:30; Ecclesiastes 3:14; Matthew 5:48)

4.There are many things that man will never fully understand in this life. In His full and complete foreknowledge, God alone has the ability to bring all things together according to His eternal plan. If man is obedient to the Word of God, this will always bring *glory to God* and *blessing to man.* (Isaiah 43:2; Romans 8:28; 2 Corinthians 12:9)

5. Our view of the events of the *present* and their concomitant consequences for the *future* is quite restricted, especially in the spirit world. God certainly has the power to defeat Satan (they are not equals!), but has given man the power of choice—a free will. Total, long-term surrender of the human will requires constant reaffirmation of faith. (Romans 8:18; 1 Peter 5:1; 2 Corinthians 4:16-18)

6. For a believer the journey of life, with all its complexities, is to be a *walk of faith*. From Abraham to Paul the holy record shouts **FAITH, FAITH, FAITH!** This is the key that unlocks each door to joyous victory in determining the appropriate passage through the oft confusing maze of daily experience.

Perhaps you have selected this book because you are in an all-consuming personal struggle with *doubt* and *fear*. The circumstance dominating your thoughts and emotions looms so large that you question if even God can do anything, or does He really care about what is happening in your life at this very moment. The simple truth is that **He does know** and **He does care**. His *mercy, grace,* and *compassion* are beyond our finest attempts to define or describe. God is greater and more powerful than the human mind can comprehend or assimilate.

For a variety of reasons, life can become very complex. In such situations there are no "quick fixes" or "Six Easy Steps" to resolving the problem. At this precise moment you may be suffering Satan's torment. He has attacked you with a barrage of emotional explosives. You are overcome with personal guilt and almost to the breaking point. This all the more reason to allow your **faith** and confident **trust** in God to sustain you until the battle subsides.

The only feasible course of action is to *run to God*, never away from Him.

• **How you can meet God through this book**

1. As you prayerfully read each chapter, allow the Holy Spirit to speak to you.

2. Come with a tender, submissive heart.

3. Do not allow your hurt to prevent you from believing.

4. Turn in your Bible to each Scripture reference. Read them carefully—the Word of God will provide *assurance, strength* and *comfort*.

   "God is our refuge and strength, a very present help in trouble" (Psalm 46:1).

   "What time I am afraid, I will trust in thee" (Psalm 56:3).

   "Casting all your care upon him, for he careth for you" (1 Peter 5:7).

Keep the faith!

H. Maurice Lednicky

CHAPTER ONE

"How Long Do You Want To Live?"

Marcia has been very active all her life. At a church function I was asked to give a one word description of my wife. I chose the word *fun*. She loves life, has a contagious smile, and has a wonderful way of making people feel comfortable. She is a great communicator and as she sings and speaks, the Lord has used her to encourage ladies all across the nation.

Let me backtrack a few years. During our college years she tried to keep an impossible schedule of academics and extra-curricular activities. The result was an hemorrhaging ulcer, which resulted in a several day stay in the hospital. The diet the doctor prescribed was simple—poached eggs three times a day. (So much for the cholesterol warning.)

Immediately after graduation from Bible college, we were traveling as evangelists. In those days the meetings often lasted two or more weeks. Quite likely the accommodations were in an "evangelists quarters" in the church, the pastor's home, or in the home of some member of the congregation. To say the least it was almost impossible to monitor her diet, not to mention the schedules for meals. The next few months presented some major challenges. Every time Marcia strayed from the bland diet, she had problems. Something as soft as mashed potatoes was out of the question. A thermos of milk was a constant companion.

On one occasion the ulcer began to hemorrhage again. We left early the next morning and drove several hours to get back to her doctor. She was so ill she lay in the back seat of the car for the whole trip. Finally, after the examination and another battery of tests, we sat in the doctor's office. He had a stern look on his face.

Marcia tentatively ventured, "How long will I have to stay on this bland diet?"

"Young lady, you decide for yourself how long you want to live." With that, he resolutely pushed himself away from his desk and walked out of the room. We were left there to ponder the seriousness of his comment.

Now I should pause to remind you that we believe in present-day miracles of divine healing. God's Word has not changed. ***Divine healing is included in the atoning provision of Christ.*.** Consequently we were diligent to pray for her healing and to ask other believers to join in faith with us.

"But he was wounded for our transgressions, he was bruised for our iniquities: the chastisement of our peace was upon him; <u>and with his stripes we are healed</u>" (Isaiah 53:5, emphasis mine).

"Is any sick among you? Let him call for the elders of the church; and let them pray over him, anointing him with oil in the name of the Lord: and <u>the prayer of faith shall save the sick, and the Lord shall raise them up</u>; and if he hath committed sins, they shall be forgiven him" (James 5:14,15, emphasis mine).

"When the even was come, they brought unto him many that were possessed with devils: and he cast out the spirits with his word, and <u>healed all that were sick</u>: that it might be fulfilled which was spoken by Esaias (Isaiah) *the prophet saying, <u>Himself took our infirmities, and bare our sickness</u>"* (Matthew 8:16,17, emphasis mine).

Some weeks after the doctor's stern admonition, Marcia picked up a book in the pastor's library. It was the biographical account of a single lady missionary who had overcome numerous obstacles in fulfilling the call of God upon her life. As she read, *Now Therefore Give Me This Mountain* (long out of print), Marcia's faith began to peak. On the way to church that evening, she said, "I believe if we will pray tonight, the Lord will heal me." Nothing new about that—we had been praying daily for more than a year.

We arrived early and went straight to the altar in the front of the sanctuary. No one else was there. Once again, we asked the Lord for divine intervention. There were no flashing lights, no thunderous voice from heaven. In fact, there was very little emotion at the moment. However, when we left the altar Marcia requested a hamburger after church that night.

I have heard all my life that honest confession is good for the soul—although, admittedly, it doesn't always help one's reputation. Still, I must confess. I knew if she were not healed we would be up all night. There was no possible way that she could eat a hamburger without major complications. But she did! She slept well and awakened the next morning without the "normal" gnawing pain in her stomach.

Lunch time came. We were eating at the pastor's home and some wonderful ladies in the church had prepared the meal. The brought in a huge spread of Mexican food. (We were down South where they really knew how to cook Mexican food.) It was hot—chili pepper hot!

In relating this marvelous testimony of divine healing, I have on occasion said that Marcia ate more of the spicy Mexican food than the rest of us. She has *suggested* that I could say, "She ate all she wanted." Incidentally, the "all she wanted" just happened to be more than anyone else. Levity aside, from that very day she has been able to eat whatever she desires. (Mexican food—the hotter the better—is still her favorite.)

This is a documented miracle. There can be no other explanation. In His sovereign plan, the Almighty extended His creative hand and restored a damaged part of her body. *If He created us in His image—He can surely heal and restore!*

THE FAITH–HEALING CONNECTION

During the earthly ministry of Jesus, He healed many people. In fact, the four biographical records (Gospels) of His life indicate He healed *"**all** manner of sickness and* *disease"* (Matthew 4:23,24; 8:16; 9:35; 12:15; 14:14,35, emphasis mine). Generally speaking, Christ's miracles of healing are collectively noted. *"So Jesus healed **great numbers** of sick people who had **many different kinds of diseases**, and he ordered many demons to come out of their victims"* (Mark 1:34, NLT, emphasis mine).

However, the Scriptures do identify numerous specific sicknesses and diseases that Christ healed. Those who were *blind, crippled (hands and feet), paralyzed, deaf, mute;* as well as those who suffered from *hemorrhaging, fever, leprosy, tumor (dropsy), convulsions,* all experienced His miraculous power to heal. Three people were *raised from the dead.* One had just died, one was being carried to the cemetery, and the other had been buried for four days. While not a physical malady as such (although some serious physical problems frequently result from it), the importance of *deliverance from demon power* cannot be overlooked.

Incidentally, *27 of the 36 recorded miracles that Christ performed while on earth relate to healing or deliverance.* This provides clear indication of the manner in which healing is interwoven into the fabric of the gospel.

Jesus came to heal the *whole person.* No one is truly well until the inner spirit has been miraculously touched by the Lord. So often He inextricably linked *spiritual* and *physical health,* both in His teaching and practice . In the case of the paralyzed man whose friends tore a hole in the roof and lowered the man into the presence of Jesus, the inspired account says, *"Seeing their faith, Jesus said to the man, 'Son, your sins are forgiven.'"* Immediately the

Pharisees and religious leaders began to protest that Jesus had no authority to forgive sins. Consequently, He turned to the paralytic and said, *"Stand up, take up your mat, and go on home, because you are healed!"* (Luke 6:17-25, NLT).

It is also interesting to observe that our Lord performed these miracles in a variety of ways. For example, to some He simply **spoke the word**; on 11 occasions He **touched the person**; three times He **spat in the process** of healing. Much to the chagrin of the Jewish religious leaders, He performed five of the healing miracles on the Sabbath. The point to be made is that Christ did not have an established pattern. Jesus did not use a prescribed *method* in healing people. What a glorious thought—He is not limited by man's *conventions, regulations*, or *assumptions*.

Although it is not noted in every miracle of healing that the Lord performed, there are several where He expressly said, *"Your faith has made you whole."* In such instances, the person himself/herself reached out in faith.

Woman with hemorrhage who touched His garment
(Matthew 9:20-22; Mark 5:25-34; Luke 8:43-48)

"Daughter, your faith has made you well. Go in peace. You have been healed" (NLT).

Two blind men
(Matthew 9:27-31)

"Because of your faith it (sight) *will happen"* (NLT).

Blind Bartimaeus
(Mark 10:46-52; Luke 18:35-43)

"Go your way. Your faith has healed you" (NLT).

Other instances involving a child or household servant also prompted the Lord to recognize the depth of faith.

Syrophoenician woman's daughter
(Matthew 15:21-28; Mark 7:24-30)

"Woman, your faith is great. Your request is granted" (NLT).

Roman officer's slave
(Luke 7:2-10)

"I tell you I haven't seen faith like this in all the land of Israel" (NLT).

Throughout the Acts account of the Early Church, miracles of healing were quite normal. One of the first major events that took place after the Day of Pentecost (birth of the Church) was the healing of the lame man who was carried daily to the Temple gate named Beautiful (Acts 3:1-10). Faith for the miraculous was at a high level as a result of how God was using the apostles. *"And by the hands of the apostles were many signs and wonders wrought among the people...Insomuch that they brought forth the sick into the streets, and laid them on beds and couches, that at least the shadow of Peter passing by might overshadow some of them"* (Acts 5:12-15). Of course, it was not some mystical act that Peter performed that produced the healing, it was the Lord Jesus Christ through him. The truth is that these sick people simply had faith they would be healed.

The apostle Paul, great apologist that he was, often saw the power of God released in physical healings. During his tenure in Ephesus, the Scripture declares, *"And God wrought special miracles by the hand of Paul: so that from his body were brought unto the sick handkerchiefs or aprons, and the diseases departed from them...*" (Acts 19:11,12). One can only conclude that it was not Peter's shadow or Paul's work aprons that brought healing. It was faith in the name of Jesus Christ who was using these servants to proclaim His resurrection power.

Faith is basic to our whole relationship with God. It is certainly not excluded or of lesser importance in matters involving physical needs in our lives. Step number one to receiving from the hand of the Almighty is believing that He is the Almighty. Never allow Satan to tantalize your mind with the *"Did God really say?"* that he hurled at Eve in the Garden of Eden. Let it be understood—*"God is not a man that he should lie. He is not a human, that he should change his mind. Has he ever spoken and failed to act? Has he ever promised and not carried it through?"* (Numbers 23:19, NLT).

• Who Prays the "PRAYER OF FAITH"?

What if those who are seriously ill or injured cannot pray? Does that mean they have no hope of healing? Absolutely not. The biblical pattern is clear. *"Is any sick among you? Let him call for the **elders** of the church; and **let them pray** over him, anointing him with oil in the name of the Lord: and the **prayer of faith** shall save the sick, and the Lord shall raise him up"* (James 5:14,15, emphasis mine).

It should be noted that the Greek word for *elders* is *presbuteros* and indicates *maturity of spiritual experience* rather than a pastoral position. The Greek word most often used to describe those who serve in leadership roles in the church is *episkopos* and is translated in English as *bishop* (overseer). This dispels the notion that only pastors or credentialed ministers can pray the *prayer of faith.*

Ample historical documentation from revival movements around the world verifies that God has often used believers who have not been called to public ministry to pray for the sick and miraculous healings have occurred.

Another vital component in our understanding of the faith-healing connection is the work of the Holy Spirit through believers. According to the instruction of Paul to the church in Corinth, the Holy Spirit administers *"spiritual gifts"* through those who are Spirit filled. Among those *"gifts"* (the list is found in 1 Corinthians 12) is the *"gifts of healing."*

There are some basic considerations for proper interpretation and understanding of this portion of Paul's letter to the Corinthians.

1. The Corinthian church was a Spirit-filled church, *"coming behind in no spiritual gift"* (1 Corinthians 1:7).

2. They were zealous for the things of God, but in many ways were carnal and immature. *"And I, brethren, could not speak unto you as spiritual, but as unto carnal, even as babes in Christ. I have fed you with milk, and not with meat: for hitherto ye were not able to bear it, neither yet now are ye able"* (1 Corinthians 3:1,2).

3. There was an apparent misunderstanding of the public ministry of the Spirit in corporate worship. Each of them was

trying to outdo the other. *"Now there are different kinds of spiritual gifts, but it is the same Holy Spirit who is the source of them all. A spiritual gift is given to each of us as a means of helping the entire church"* (1 Corinthians 12:4,7, NLT).

4. The *"gifts of the Spirit"* are resident in the Spirit; the Spirit is resident within the believer. Consequently, it is the *work* and *will* of the Holy Spirit that determines when and through whom such gifts will be manifested. *"It is the one and only Holy Spirit who distributes these gifts. He alone decides which gift each person should have"* (1 Corinthians 12:11, NLT).

There is no scriptural indication that the ministry of the Holy Spirit has been altered or ceased since the founding of the New Testament church.

At some point in time, for some specific need, the Holy Spirit may call upon you (or any Spirit-filled believer) to be the channel through which the healing virtue of Christ will flow into the body of someone who desperately needs a miracle. What at awesome thought! Never be a spectator at prayer time. Never be casual or unconcerned. *Your released faith could very well be the catalyst that God uses to heal a diseased, dissipated, or afflicted body.*

• **In His Time**

One of the constant challenges of faith is to add a

healthy dose of patience. When we pray and believe—we *expect* God to answer right now. More about this later. A comment or two at this moment will be sufficient.

1. There is no implication that faith is weak or faulty because God does not respond to the petition immediately. Don't allow the devil or anyone else to hammer you over the head with this unscriptural teaching.

2. One should never feel guilty for *persistently* and *repeatedly asking* for an answer to the same need. It has been said that if you ask for the same thing twice, you did not have faith the first time you asked. This is exactly opposite of what the Lord Jesus taught. Read the Gospel of Luke—the devotional gospel which has a strong emphasis on prayer, with many of the Lord's prayers detailed. In Chapter 11, He tells a parable of a man who wanted to borrow some food at midnight. The friend will not get up on the basis of friendship, but he does because of the man's persistence. Then, Jesus said, *"And so I tell you, keep on asking, and you will be given what you ask for. Keep on looking, and you will find. Keep on knocking, and the door will be opened. For everyone who asks, receives. Everyone who seeks, finds. And the door is opened to everyone who knocks"* (Luke 11:9,10, NLT).

Jesus Christ is the healer. No theological or intellectual excuses will alter the Word of God. We are made in His own image—certainly He can heal and restore His creation!

11

CHAPTER TWO

"I Loaned Her To You"

Mischelle, our only child, came home from an overnight Girl Scout campout with a stomachache. *Too many hot dogs, too little sleep,* we reasoned. Nothing to be overly concerned about. After all, she loved the outdoors and had probably pushed herself to the limit. She collected rocks and so I had brought her unusual rocks from all over the world. At age eight she had wanted a baseball bat and glove for her birthday. She enjoyed fast-paced team activites.

But, the pain persisted. So did a low grade fever. The doctor diagnosed a kidney infection. After taking the prescribed dose of antibiotics, both the pain and the fever were still present. A visit to the pediatrician who had delivered her nine years earlier created even greater concern. On to Texas Children's Hospital (Houston) for tests and finally to St. Jude's Children's Hospital (Memphis, Tennessee). The diagnosis was devastating. Missy had a rare type of leukemia. According to medical journals, no one had lived as long as two years with this unusual form of leukemia.

What followed was 16 months of intense agonizing before the Lord for her healing. People all around the world prayed for her. There is absolutely no question in my mind—Mischelle had faith; Marcia and I and the rest of the family had faith; the congregation we were serving had faith; ministerial colleagues and believers that we knew in many nations had faith. But, in the *sovereign providence* of a good, gracious, loving God, He promoted Mischelle from *earthly life* to *eternal life.*

Along this difficult journey, there were some powerful and priceless moments. Mischelle was a very beautiful young lady with a sweet disposition and winning personality, relating well both to her peers and adults. Her love for Christ was evident. She was deeply involved in every activity of the church—Sunday School, children's choir, Missionettes (girls group)—that was available to her.

One evening at the dinner table, a career missionary, who was home on furlough to attend seminary, and I were discussing the scriptural truth of *divine healing.* Missy was sitting quietly at the table listening to the conversation. In a few moments she said, "Dad," and I responded, "Just a minute, Babe, Dad's talking right now." This happened another time or two and finally I said, "What did you want to say?" Quietly she offered, "Dad, you know that God heals all of His children. Some here on earth; others when they get to heaven." End of theological discussion. Profoundly, this nine-year-old had distilled the eternal truth in two concise sentences.

As time was progressing and the medical attempts were apparently not effective, Marcia said, "Missy, we believe that Jesus can heal you. What would you think if we decided not to take any more of the treatments and just trust Him for your healing?" She silently thought for a few moments before she responded and then said, "Oh, Mom, that would be wonderful. But how do we know that God is through showing the doctors and nurses what He wants them to see in my life?" As we look back now, there is no doubt that the Lord was giving this little mind insights that were far beyond her years.

On Monday, December 15, Mischelle had a splenectomy and exploratory surgery. She had a vertical incision of almost seven inches on her frail frame. The doctor told her that she might be able to be at home for Christmas. The next Sunday morning (December 21) she was in church—and sang "To God Be the Glory."

A few days later when she went back to see the surgeon, Missy proudly told him that she had sung on Sunday. He was a wonderful Christian brother in his early sixties. So, he asked her what she had sung. "To God Be the Glory," she replied. "I know that one," the doctor said and began to quote the words of the first verse. "To God be the glory, great things He has done..." Mischelle interrupted, "That's not the song I sang, but I know that one too." So, together, this renowned surgeon and frail little ten-year-old stood in his office and vibrantly lifted their voices and sang.

"To God be the glory, great things He has done,
So loved He the world that He gave us His Son.
Who yielded His life as a ransom for sin,
And opened the lifegate that all may go in.
Praise the Lord, Praise the Lord,
Let the earth hear His voice.
Praise the Lord, Praise the Lord,
Let the people rejoice.
O come to the Father, through Jesus the Son,
And give Him the glory, great things He has done."

Several nurses were crowded into the doorway listening. There was not a dry eye. As we walked back through the patient waiting area, the 20 or more people sitting there were in complete silence. God was indeed using this young lady to give Him glory.

We determined that we would not keep anything from Mischelle, so she fully understood that outside of divine intervention, she could die. Although she suffered (with more than 30 bone marrow tests, exploratory surgery, chemo, blood transfusions), she was never afraid. To her, "going to be with Jesus was a happy time." And when it appeared that the moment for her departure from earthly life had arrived, our family gathered around her bed in isolation intensive care and joined hands together and prayed. Marcia leaned over the bed and whispered in her ear. "Missy, you remember that you said that Jesus heals all His children, either here or in heaven. This is your day for healing and we believe that Jesus is coming to take you to be with Him. Mom will go with you as far as I can, then Jesus will come and take you by the hand and lead you the rest of the way." Although she could not respond, it was as though she breathed a sigh of relief and in a few moments she was in the presence of the Lord.

Was that experience difficult? Far more than I could ever describe. There is only one resource that can hold you on a emotionally steady course during such devastating events of this life—*faith in Almighty God*. The God we serve is *good, gracious*, and *loving*. He is not some vindictive tyrant trying to force his subjects to grovel in the dirt.

"The Lord is like a father to his children, tender and compassionate to those who fear him. For he understands how weak we are; he knows we are only dust" (Psalm 103:13,14, NLT).

"The Lord is kind and merciful, slow to get angry, full of unfailing love" (Psalm 145:8, NLT).

"If you sinful people know how to give good gifts to your children, how much more will your heavenly father give good gifts to those who ask him" (Matthew 7:11, NLT).

"Whatever is good and perfect comes to us from God above, who created all heaven's lights. Unlike them, he never changes or casts shifting shadows. In his goodness he chose to make us his own children by giving us his true word. And we, out of all creation, became his choice possession" (James 1:17,18, NLT).

Missy was buried on Wednesday and we went away for a few days, but returned on Saturday to fill the pulpit on Sunday. In the Monday morning mail, we received a letter that has dramatically impacted our lives. Incidentally, the stamp was canceled, but there was no location noted as to where the letter came from.

This letter is *very personal*, and we share it to emphasize that our Heavenly Father is a *very personal God*. You will note the line that says, "This letter is not to be shared with the world. It is for you two alone". For some time we struggled with the meaning of this and did not show the letter to anyone. However, after seeking the Lord, we came to the conclusion that this means of "speaking" must never be viewed as a *model* or *method*. Perhaps others have received similar expressions on occasion; however, I want to be clear. I am in no way suggesting that God will communicate again in this manner to us or to others. He may or may not choose to do so. That is His prerogative. Further, while I sincerely believe that this missive was from the Lord, it must never be assumed that it is equal to the Word of God.

To: The Earthly Parents of Mischelle Louise Lednicky

Today, as you return to the earth that little casement which held the one you called "Mischelle" you are still wanting to ask Me why. This is how I have of answering you. You are to accept this without question for the person being used by Me is but another servant and is merely doing My bidding. You have never seen, nor do you know, the one of whom I speak.

Behold, I am the Lord thy God, and beside Me there is none else.

In the days ahead of you, there will be lonely hours, such as you sometime think you cannot bear. It is at these times you are to take the Word of God and go alone to your secret prayer closet and you are to meet Me there. I will strengthen thee, yea, I will help thee; yea, I will uphold thee by the right hand of My righteousness. Behold, I the Lord, thy God, have spoken.

This letter is not to be shared with the world. It is for you two alone. I commend you for the loving care you bestowed on My little Mischelle Louise. You see, Children, it is far better this way. <u>*I loaned her to you so that you could get to know Me better. This purpose has been accomplished. I had no intention of leaving her on earth any longer than that*</u> *(emphasis mine). You are to lift your hands and hearts in praise to Me. I have loved you with an everlasting love. Your Heavenly Father knows what is best for you, My beloved children. Maurice, you will go forth and preach a stronger message because of this refining fire I have seen fit to endow you with. In My strength, in My might you will walk anew. You are to proclaim the gospel of My salvation to a lost and dying world. Be thou faithful unto death and I shall have a crown laid up for you at the end of that time.*

Lift up your hearts, O My Children, and praise the Lord for I, the Lord thy God, have heard thy cries, I know thy aching hearts, I feel thy grief and I tell you that I am the Giver of Life and I am the Sustainer of the soul.

Behold, I am the Lord thy God and beside Me there is NONE else.

Does this mean that we are to denounce all emotional pain and grief when we face the trials of this life?

Absolutely not. In coming to grips with the biblical perspective on this issue, the Lord clearly spoke to my heart. We are *created in His image* and He is a God of *love*. We would not be like Christ (God manifested in the flesh), if we did not express love. Love is an emotion that may manifest itself in either joy or sorrow. Both are legitimate expressions of the Creator, and thus of those created in His image.

According to the Gospels, Christ was *"moved with compassion"* for the **multitudes** (Matthew 9:36; 14:14); for the **unfortunate** (Matthew 20:34); for the **sick/diseased** (Mark 1:41); and for the **bereaved** (Luke 7:13; John 11:35). At the tomb of Lazarus, *"Jesus wept,"* and those standing nearby commented, *"See how much he loved him"* (John 11:35,36).

> *"For we do not have a high priest who is unable to sympathize with our weaknesses, but we have one who has been tempted in every way, just as we are—yet without sin. Let us then approach the throne of grace with confidence, so that we may receive mercy and find grace to help us in our time of need"* (Hebrews 4:15,16, NIV).

The pain caused by the death of a family member or close friend (who is a born-again believer) is not sorrow for them, but rather for the separation we experience. At that moment, we can neither express love nor receive love from that individual. The Bible specifically addresses this in Paul's effort to encourage and assure the believers at Thessalonica that those who had died in the faith would be resurrected at the coming of the Lord. *"But I would not have you to be ignorant, brethren, concerning them which are asleep, <u>that ye sorrow not, even as others which have</u>*

no hope" (1 Thessalonians 4:1, emphasis mine). This passage does not condemn our grief in processing the death of a loved one. What it, however, does condemn is an absence of faith. Remember, our hope is an eternal one and to deport ourselves as those who consider death as a final separation, is nothing less than unbelief in the finished work of the Cross. For the child of God *death is never punishment—it is always promotion.*

• The Two Sides of Faith

Broken down in the most simplistic terms, one side of faith reflects the <u>miraculous intervention</u> of deity in human circumstance when the <u>God-given answer</u> exactly overlays the <u>petition</u> that was presented before Him. The other side of faith stipulates that we must <u>maintain confidence</u> in His <u>sovereign wisdom</u> when the <u>God-given answer</u> does not correspond to the <u>petition</u> that was presented before Him.

By relating Marcia's experience of divine healing (Chapter One) and Mischelle's illness and death, I have attempted to anecdotally establish the basic premise for this volume—***balancing your faith with God's sovereignty.*** To be certain, there are no over-the-counter, quick-fix, seven-easy-steps kinds of answers. And, it is this fact that makes faith such a key issue in our relationship with the Almighty. Every situation is unique. God's plans for His children are not machine made. He knows each of us individually and has masterfully crafted a personal blueprint for each life. His way is *always right and good!* Never, ever doubt it.

• Being Angry with God—and Other Foolish Notions

From time to time someone will ask, "Aren't you angry at God about this?" Without question it is always acceptable to tell God just what and how you feel—for after all, our kind, caring Father knows the pain and hurts we encounter. However, to remain angrily hostile toward His plan for an indefinite period of time becomes, at the very least, a statement of spiritual immaturity for a true believer. To one who has been a follower of Christ for many years and knows the Word of God, it may even border on sacrilege.

Very seldom is man's anger acceptable. Paul, in urging unity in the Ephesian church, says, *"And don't sin by letting anger gain control over you. Don't let the sun go down while you are still angry, for anger gives a mighty foothold to the Devil"* (Ephesians 4:26,27, NLT). If this reference addresses the matter of human relationships, how much more should it apply to the restored relationship with the Father through the redemptive work of Christ in our behalf.

While ministering in a local church on Sunday night, I noticed a gentleman with whom I had been friends for many years. In fact, for a short time we had been room-mates during our Bible college days. He sat on the back pew with a scowl on his face during the entire service. At the conclusion of the message, I went back to greet him and offer to pray with him. He said something like, "You don't have time to listen to me." I responded that I did have the time and would like to talk with him. Finally, rather abruptly, he quipped, "OK, I don't like the way God treats me!"

I called him by name and asked if he remembered our

daughter Mischelle. The last time he had seen her she would have been five or six years old. He nodded that he did. I said sometimes Mischelle will come into the house all excited and want me to buy a certain thing for her. I know it would not be the best for her to have whatever she was asking for at that time. At her young age, she does not always understand the reasoning of her parents. Even though she is disappointed, as her father I have the responsibility to do what is best for her. Then I posed this question. "Do you think that in her few years of life, she has more knowledge and wisdom than her parents? Does she have the maturity to determine what is best for her and how such a decision would impact her life?"

He shook his head in agreement that simply by reason of age and experience she could not always make the best choices. I then turned the question to him. "What would cause you to believe that you have greater wisdom in decision making about your life than your Heavenly Father? On what basis could any of us ever come to such a conclusion?" At that moment he began to weep and turned and knelt beside the pew in deep repentance. I have a cherished letter from my friend saying that that night was "a turning point in his life after several years of wandering in the wilderness."

God is a good God—He wants the best for us.

Never allow Satan to confuse your mind with some ridiculous notion that the Heavenly Father loves someone else more than He loves you.

Our view is so limited. Instead of being angry with God, we should ever be grateful to Him for guiding our lives along a pathway that allows us to fulfill the purpose He has arranged for this earthly journey.

Then there is the old *que sera, sera* song. Whatever will be, will be, so what difference does it make anyway? If God is sovereign, then why bother to pray or have faith? He *will* have it His own way. What a distorted picture of God and His desire for man. ***Prayer coupled with faith is never offensive to the Sovereign One***. The admonition of Scripture is to *"keep on asking."* Only, and the emphasis is on the word only, if the Holy Spirit directly addresses a specific issue should you cease to earnestly seek the Lord with a particular request.

Such instances are rarely found in Scripture. **Moses pled with God to enter the Promised Land.** *"At that time I pleaded with the Lord and said, 'O Sovereign Lord, I am your servant. Please let me cross the Jordan to see the wonderful land on the other side...' But the Lord was angry with me because of you, and he would not listen to me. 'That's enough!' he ordered. 'Speak of it no more. You may go to Pisgah Peak and view the land in every direction, but you may not cross the Jordan River'"* (Deuteronomy 3:23-27, NLT, emphasis mine).

The **apostle Paul prayed to be delivered from a** *"thorn in the flesh."* *"But to keep me from getting puffed up, I was given a thorn in my flesh, a messenger from Satan to torment me and keep me from getting proud. Three different times I begged the Lord to take it away. Each time he said, 'My gracious favor is all you need. My power works* *best in weakness.' So now I am glad to boast about my weakness, so that the power of Christ may work through me"* (2 Corinthians 12:7-9, NLT, emphasis mine).

The simple truth is that we do not and cannot think like God. It is impossible for the finite to comprehend the infinite. *"'My thoughts are completely different from yours,' says the Lord. 'And my ways are far beyond anything you can imagine. For just as the heavens are higher than the earth, so are my ways higher than your ways and my thoughts higher than your thoughts'"* (Isaiah 55:8,9, NLT).

Paul sums it up so magnificently in the Book of Romans. *"Oh, what a wonderful God we have! How great are his riches and wisdom and knowledge! How impossible for us to understand his decisions and his methods!"* (Romans 11:33, NLT). Notice the exclamation point at the conclusion to all three sentences. It appears that the apostle Paul was quite excited at this point.

Dear saint of the Most High, when your heart is crushed by the inexplicable and you have no more tears to shed, tighten your grip of faith on the hand of the One who has promised to see you safely through the valley. *"When they walk through the Valley of Weeping, it will become a place of refreshing springs, where pools of blessing collect after the rains!"* (Psalm 84:6, NLT).

> *"Some through the water, some through the flood,*
> *Some through the fire, but all through the Blood.*
> *Some through great sorrow, but God gives a song,*
> *In the night season, and all the day long."*

CHAPTER THREE

The Three Hebrew Boys Were Right

It is one of the most dramatic scenes in the Bible. Three young captives defying the command of the ruler of the world empire. The consequence was immediate punishment. Not just being dragged into court or imprisonment, but death by being thrown into a blazing hot furnace. We have the inspired record that reveals the victorious outcome of their refusal to compromise their faith—but remember they *did not know* what was going to happen. The probing question is, How would you or I react to a similar crisis?

Just to have the details of this event, let's review the account from the Book of Daniel. A bit of background is helpful before we look at Chapter Three. The Southern Kingdom (Judah) had been invaded by the Babylonians under the leadership of King Nebuchadnezzar. **Jeremiah** the prophet had been warning of this coming invasion for many years, but the people did not listen to the *weeping* *prophet.* Instead, they wanted to hear a message of *peace and prosperity.* (Somehow that has a familiar sound to it.)

A number of Jewish people were taken captive and God raised up **Ezekiel** to minister to these POWs in Babylon. But King Nebuchadnezzar was quite crafty in his strategy of world rulership. So, he found some of the brightest young minds and sent them to university for a first-class education. Those selected (by IQ or some entrance exam?) were to be taught *"the language and literature of the Babylonians"* (Daniel 1:4, NLT) for a *"three year period, and then some of them would be made advisers in the royal court"* (Daniel 1:5, NLT). Among those who were entered into the university program were Daniel, Hananiah, Mishael, and Azariah. Of course, **Daniel** became the prophet/statesman that God anointed to speak from this worldwide platform.

Hananiah, Mishael, and Azariah are more likely to be known to us as **Shadrach, Meshach,** and **Abednego**. Following their graduation they were placed in the royal court *"to be in charge of all the affairs of the province of Babylon"* (Daniel 2:49, NLT). As significant as it may have been for these Jewish captives to be appointed to such positions of authority, it is their ***uncompromising expression of faith*** that finds its way into scriptural record.

King Nebuchadnezzar built a 90 feet tall golden statue of himself (pride is an awful sin) and demanded that everyone, including the Jewish captives, bow down to worship. *"People of all races and nations and languages, listen to the king's command! When you hear the sound of the horn, flute, zither, lyre, harp, and other instruments, bow to the ground to worship King Nebuchadnezzar's gold statue. Anyone who refuses to obey will immediately be thrown into a blazing furnace"* (Daniel 3:4-6, NLT).

When Shadrach, Meshach, and Abednego refused to worship the golden statue, some jealous want-to-bes ran to the king to tattle. Nebuchadnezzar *"flew into a rage"* (Daniel 3:13, NLT) and ordered the three to come before him immediately. Now here is where the spiritual battle is pitched. Ultimately, *all challenges to faith are in the spiritual realm*. Although it may (and most likely will) be fought in the arena of human experience, the actual conflict is to determine which "god" will govern our allegiance.

"I will give you one more chance. If you bow down and worship the statue I have made...all will be well. But if you refuse, you will be thrown immediately into the blazing furnace. <u>What god will be able to rescue you from my power then?</u>" (Daniel 3:15, NLT, emphasis mine).

Watch their answer. This is no longer political. This is not a matter of ruler-subject dominance. This has now openly become *god* versus *God*. *"O Nebuchadnezzar, we do not need to defend ourselves before you. If we are thrown into the blazing furnace, <u>the God whom we serve is able to save us</u>. <u>He will rescue us from your power, Your Majesty</u>. But <u>even if he doesn't</u>, Your Majesty, can be sure that we will <u>never serve your gods or worship the golden statue</u> you have set up"* (Daniel 3:16-18, NLT, emphasis mine).

Of course, we know the victorious climax to this story. Nebuchadnezzar became so *"furious that his face became distorted with rage"* and he commanded that the *"furnace be heated seven times hotter than usual"* (Daniel 3:19, NLT). In today's vernacular, we would say that he "lost it." Shadrach, Meshach, and Abednego were thrown into the furnace, but were not consumed in the raging inferno. In fact, *not a hair on their heads was singed, and their clothing was not scorched. They didn't even smell of smoke!"* (Daniel 3:27, NLT).

Back to the spiritual nature of this faith challenge. The king is so angry at their refusal to worship his image that he is personally watching to see these disloyal captives burn to death. Suddenly, he jumped to his feet in amazement. *"Didn't we tie up three men and throw them into the furnace? I see <u>four men</u>, unbound, walking around in the fire. They aren't even hurt by the flames! And the <u>fourth looks like a divine being</u>"* (Daniel 3:24, 25, NLT, emphasis mine). The Aramaic is more literally translated *"looks like a son of the gods."* The King James translation reads: *"the form of the fourth is like the Son of God."* While there is no scriptural indication that Nebuchadnezzar accepted the One True God at this time (you need to read Daniel 4 to hear his final recorded statements), he did issue a decree that no one was to *"speak a word against the God of Shadrach, Meshach, and Abednego...There is no other god who can rescue like this!"* (Daniel 3:29, NLT).

This miracle of deliverance is exciting; however, to uncover the full depth of how this relates to the whole subject of faith, we must probe a bit deeper into the Scripture. It is truly amazing that the profound can become quite clear as the Holy Spirit illuminates the Word and, in doing so, makes the appropriate application to our lives today.

THE TWO INDISPENSABLE ELEMENTS OF FAITH

Confidence in God's Omnipotence

"Our God is able to deliver us..."

Trust in God's Omniscience

"But if not..."

It is not an either-or with God. He is both **omnipotent** (*all powerful*) and **omniscient** (*all knowing/wise*). These divine attributes are neither in conflict nor competition with each other. Both are manifestations of absolute perfection expressed in flawless harmony.

The believer with a healthy, mature faith will embrace this marvelous scriptural truth, whether in times of joyous victory or bitter trial. There must be caution that we do attempt to play one against the other. As we shall examine later, *the maturity of one's faith is not to be measured exclusively by results, nor is it measured exclusively by resignation.*

In considering the **omnipotence of God**, let's begin at the beginning—as far as the human mind can comprehend. This is not an extensive treatment of this subject; however, numerous scriptural references will be noted. As a reminder, it is the Word of God alone that is the solid rock foundation upon which true faith is built. *"So then faith cometh by hearing, and hearing by the word of God"* (Romans 10:17).

1. God is self-existent (Genesis 1:1; Exodus 3:13,14)

2. God is eternal (Deuteronomy 33:27; Psalm 145:13; Revelation 1:8)

3. God is self-sufficient (Psalm 50:7-12; Isaiah 40:9-28; Romans 11:34-36)

4. God is infinite (Psalm 19:8; Isaiah 66:1; Jeremiah 23:24)

5. God is creator of all things (Genesis 1-2; Nehemiah 9:6; Colossians 1:16; Revelation 4:11)

On this strategic matter of divine creation (it is frequently denied in educational circles), there is a popular New Age school of thought that seeks to integrate God with nature. What an insult to the God who *"spoke the worlds into existence."* God's relationship with nature as defined in Scripture is quite clear.

1. God created nature (Colossians 1:16)

2. God upholds nature (Colossians 1:17)

3. God transcends nature (Psalm 90:2; 102:25-27)

4. God is immanent in nature (Ephesians 1:11)

5. God has a purpose in nature (Ephesians 1:9-11)

6. God uses nature as a means to reveal Himself to man (Romans 1:19,20)

There are numerous miracles in both Old and New

Testaments that speak eloquently to God's transcendence of His creation. Long ago I came to the conclusion anything that God touches is supernatural.

Israel crossing the Red Sea on dry ground (Exodus 14)

The sun "stood still" during battle (Joshua 10)

Daniel delivered from the hungry lions (Daniel 6)

Christ calming the storm on the Sea of Galilee (Matthew 8; Mark 4; Luke 8)

The disciples having a miraculous catch of fish (Luke 5)

From the creation of the universe and man until the final overthrow of Satan and the investiture of the eternal kingdom, God is in control. Generally speaking, believers have faith that the Almighty has a *master plan* and the various components will eventually fall into place. However, with the complexities of the present-day world, (unfortunately) some believers have even questioned if God has the power to solve such horrific events. *Never, never doubt—He has the power!*

The tempter comes against most of us in ways which relate to personal matters. A physical malady or a financial crisis or a major family dilemma often severely challenges our faith. I quickly come back to Shadrach, Meshach, and Abednego—staring a furious ruler and horrible death right in the face—they emphatically, positively declared, *"Our God is able to deliver us."* Their God was personally concerned and involved in this circumstance. They knew He had the power to overrule the authority of King Nebuchadnezzar. That is *faith in action.*

The first giant step toward living is spiritual victory is an unwavering declaration of confidence in God's power to alter any circumstance.

DOUBT AND FEAR ARE HINDRANCES TO FAITH
DOUBT QUESTIONS IF GOD CAN
FEAR QUESTIONS IF GOD WILL

This may be an appropriate moment to quietly and honestly open the private rooms of your heart. Allow the Word and Spirit to speak directly to you. Are there *doubts* about God's power to move your mountain? The writer of Hebrews clearly stipulates the order for our faith to be effective. *"So, you see, it is impossible to please God without faith. Anyone who wants to come to him <u>must believe</u> <u>that there is a God</u> and that he sincerely rewards those who seek him"* (Hebrews 11:6, NLT).

Now, let's consider the *"But if not…"* aspect of faith. It almost sounds contradictory. How can you believe for the impossible and at the same time be as resoundingly emphatic about the "if He chooses not to deliver"? This is pivotal to understanding the scriptural truth of *balancing your faith with God's sovereignty.* It is here and only here that we can be assured of victory under any and every circumstance.

This was not a cop-out. These men were not looking for a back door—just in case. There was no hint of "if our faith is weak" or some other facing-saving explanation. Shadrach, Meshach, and Abebnego were saying, "Not only do we have unconditional confidence in God's power to do the utterly impossible, we also place total trust in His wisdom to make the right decision in this situation."

In the Book of Proverbs, Solomon speaks extensively of the importance of *wisdom*. You will recall that his petition to the Lord was to have *"an understanding heart to judge thy people, that I may discern between good and bad"* (1 Kings 3:5-13).

I am intrigued by the wording of Proverbs 3:19, *"The Lord by wisdom hath founded the earth; by understanding hath he established the heavens."* Why didn't he say, "The Lord by His mighty power created the earth and heavens"? Suddenly it dawned on me. To Solomon, the power of God was a given. But the Sovereign One did not simply use raw power in creation. He wisely—with intricate plan and eternal purpose—used His power. And, so He does in the daily events of life in each of His children. Indeed, *"The steps of the godly are directed by the Lord. He delights in every detail of their lives"* (Psalm 37:23, NLT).

If one does not experientially connect **confidence in God's power** with **trust in God's wisdom**, there will be an interminable assortment of questions about event after event in life. Quite likely at the head of most lists will be **Why?**.

Let's look at another example from the Bible. King Herod put the apostle James to death. When he did so, *"he saw that it pleased the Jews."* Consequently, he imprisoned the apostle Peter and intended to bring him to public trial. On the night before this trial, Peter was miraculously delivered from prison. It is a fascinating story. He was chained between two soldiers and 14 others were standing guard at the prison gate. By the way, the apostle was sound asleep. An angel awakened Peter and led him through the prison gate, and the city gate. When he realized that he was not dreaming, he headed straight to church. (There should be a lesson here for us.) Read the details in Acts 12.

The point here is not about God's power to perform this miraculous deliverance. Rather, it is about His sovereign plan. Could God have just as easily delivered the apostle James from the clutches of King Herod? The obvious answer is yes. However, if we fail to link His sovereign wisdom with His power, we soon begin to question God. Such human thought patterns as *God has favorites* or *it just doesn't seem fair* begin to slip into the conversation.

As the believer develops this mature understanding of faith, an unexplainable peace begins to override normally anxious emotions. In his beautiful letter of thanks to the saints at Philippi for their sacrificial generosity, Paul urges, *"Always be full of joy in the Lord. I say it again—rejoice!"*. In the King James translation, the words *"joy"* and *"rejoice"* are used almost 20 times. The admonition that follows these words is both challenging and comforting. *"Don't worry about anything; instead pray about everything. Tell God what you need, and thank him for all he has done. If you do this, you will experience God's peace, which is far more wonderful than the human mind can understand. His peace will guard your hearts and minds as you live in Christ Jesus*" (Philippians 4:6, 7, NLT, emphasis mine).

Remember, this is not a textbook theology. Paul is in prison again. He knew what it was to have life turned upside down. With the powerful voice of personal experience to authenticate his instruction, he spoke. Incidentally, the Greek word for *guard* that is used here (under divine inspiration) means to *"hem in, protect as with a garrison."* Also, it is quite significant that he mentions both *"heart"* (feelings, emotions) and *"mind"* (thoughts, intellect). It is at these two points our faith is most vulnerable to the accusations of Satan.

MAJOR CHALLENGES TO OUR FAITH ARE MOST LIKELY TO COME IN AREAS THAT TEST OUR WILLINGNESS TO TRUST IN GOD'S SOVEREIGN WISDOM .

Living under the constant pressure of *distressed emotions* and *confused thoughts* will eventually damage or destroy the supernatural peace that God has promised His children.

The Word of God provides such marvelous counsel.

"You will keep in perfect peace all who trust in you, whose thoughts are fixed on you! Trust in the Lord always, for the Lord God is the eternal Rock" (Isaiah 26:3,4, NLT).

"Trust in the Lord with all your heart; do not depend on your own understanding" (Proverbs 3:5, NLT).

Lest you feel condemned or confused, be certain that this is no easy task. It does not happen with one life lesson—it is a life-long process. Do not be discouraged if you seem to be clinging to a rope swinging back and forth between faith and fear. Always remember that **God is a good God**. He desires the very best for you—He knows what is best. This is where *confidence in His power* and *trust in His wisdom* must link together arm in arm. **Victory is certain—by faith!**

CHAPTER FOUR

What Does Sovereign Mean?

By dictionary definition, **sovereign** means "(1) *above or superior to all others; chief; greatest; supreme*, (2) *supreme in power, rank, or authority*." While we can mentally grasp the meaning of the words, it is most difficult to fully comprehend the essence of their significance, relevance, and consequence in our relationship with the One True God.

For a poignant real-life lesson, let's visit King Nebuchadnezzar again. Remember, he was ruler of the world empire. In the book of Daniel (Chapter 2), the Babylonian leader had a strange dream and then could not recall what he had dreamed. He demanded that his *"wise men"* tell him what he had dreamed and what it meant. Even those who normally would not question his authority became frustrated.

"The astrologers replied to the king, 'There isn't a man alive who can tell Your Majesty his dream! And no king,

however great and powerful, has ever asked such a thing of any magician, enchanter, or astrologer! This is an impossible thing that the king requires. No one except the gods can tell you your dream, and they do not live among people'" (Daniel 2:10,11, NLT).

The king was furious at their response, and he did what men in his position do when someone makes them angry. *"He sent out orders to execute all the wise men of Babylon"* (Daniel 2:12, NLT). The decree included Daniel, Shadrach, Meshach, and Abednego. But, God revealed the dream to Daniel. He was able to tell the king what he had dreamed and then give the proper interpretation.

"Your Majesty, in your vision you saw in front of you a huge and powerful statue of a man, shining brilliantly, frightening and awesome. The <u>head of the statue was made of fine gold</u>, its chest and arms were of silver, its belly and thighs were of brass, its legs were of iron, and its feet were a combination of iron and clay" (Daniel 2:31-33, NLT, emphasis mine).

"Your Majesty, you are a king over many kings. <u>The God of heaven has given you sovereignty, power, strength, and honor</u>. He has made you ruler over all the inhabited world and has put even the animals and birds under your control. <u>You are the head of gold</u>" (Daniel 2:36-38, NLT, emphasis mine).

This, of course, is a revelation of the world empires, as they would historically rise, beginning with Babylon. However, the prophetically relevant message is that *"a rock was cut from the mountain by supernatural means"* and it struck the image on the feet and *"the whole statue col-lapsed into a heap of iron, clay, bronze, silver, and gold"* (Daniel 2:34,35, NLT). There is little doubt that this is a direct reference to the coming Kingdom of Christ Jesus. You may wish to give more careful study to this prophetic passage than can be afforded here.

In due time, King Nebuchadnezzar had another dream. This time Daniel explained about a huge tree *"growing very tall and strong, reaching high into the heavens for all the world to see"* (Daniel 4:20, NLT). Again, with God-given insight, Daniel explained, *"That tree, Your Majesty, is you. For you have grown strong and great; your greatness reach-es up to heaven, and your rule to the ends of the earth"* (Daniel 4:22, NLT). Unfortunately, the tree was to be cut down to the ground, with only the stump remaining. And, sure enough the great king became so proud and arrogant that Almighty God sent him into the fields to eat grass like a cow for seven years. His hair grew long like an eagle's feathers and his fingernails like birds' claws. What a incred-ulous shock this must have been to the world.

Why am I belaboring this point? From the standpoint of human position and authority, King Nebuchadnezzar was the greatest on earth at that time. By man's definition he was a sovereign ruler. But, in no way did he compare to the Sovereign God of all ages.

Now, hear his confession at the end of this seven-year period of exile. *"My sanity returned, and I praised and worshipped the Most High and honored the one who lives forever. His rule is everlasting, and his kingdom is eternal.*

All the people of the earth are nothing compared to him. He has the <u>power to do as he pleases</u> among the angels of heaven and with those who live on earth. Now I, Nebuchadnezzar, <u>praise and glorify and honor the King of heaven</u>. All his acts are just and true, and he is able to humble those who are proud" (Daniel 4:34-37, NLT, emphasis mine).

This is no lowly, impoverished servant speaking. This man has literally "had it all." He possessed raw, unrestrained power. He wallowed in incredible wealth. But, today he confesses that there is none like the Sovereign King of heaven!

Perhaps it would be appropriate for us to look at another aspect of divine sovereignty. The Old Testament book of Habakkuk reveals the prophet's deep frustration. He is boldly (angrily?) questioning the wisdom of the Sovereign God in how He is treating His own chosen people.

Chapter 1:1-4   **Habakkuk's complaint**

"How long, O Lord, must I call for help? But you do not listen! 'Violence!' I cry, but you do not come to save. Must I forever see this sin and misery around me?" (vv. 2,3, NLT).

Chapter 1:5-11   **God's response**

"Watch and be astounded at what I will do! For I am doing something in your own day, something you wouldn't believe even if someone told you about it. I am raising up the Babylonians to be a new power on the world scene. They are a cruel and violent nation who will

march across the world and conquer it" (vv. 5,6, NLT).

Chapter 1:12-17   **Habakkuk's confusion**

"O Lord my God, my Holy One, you who are eternal—is your plan in all this to wipe us (Jewish people) *out? Surely not! O Lord our Rock, you have decreed the rise of these Babylonians to punish and correct us for our terrible sins. <u>You are perfectly just in this</u>. But will you, who cannot allow sin in any form, stand idly by while they swallow us up? <u>Should you be silent while the wicked destroy people who are more righteous than they?</u>"* (vv. 12,13, NLT, emphasis mine).

Is this a valid question? From the standpoint of human reason, perhaps it could be. However, we must not forget that in keeping with God's holiness, His people have committed the most horrific of all sins—they were worshipping other gods. (Remember the First Commandment?) This was unacceptable for these Babylonians or any other pagans, but it was unthinkable for these monotheistic Jews.

Chapter 2:2-20   **God's clarification of His plan**

"But these things won't happen right away. Slowly, steadily, surely, the time approaches when the vision will be fulfilled. <u>If it seems slow, wait patiently for it, for it will surely take place</u>" (v. 3, NLT, emphasis mine).

God intended to use the Babylonians to punish the Jewish people for their disobedience and idol worship. Then, in His perfect timing, He would turn and punish the Babylonians for the many evils they had committed. Moral judgment upon the sins of man will take place—you can be certain of it. This message to the prophet seems especially apropos for this self-justifying generation.

As believers, we want God to rise up and destroy all evil around us immediately. Be assured, dear saint, that God has not lost the way. In due time—exactly according to the eternal "clock"—His justice will prevail.

Included in this passage is the verse that has become the watchword for all true believers. *"The just shall live by faith"* (v. 4). This verse is quoted three times in the New Testament (Romans 1:17; Galatians 3:11, Hebrews 10:38). Other translations indicate the word *"faith"* is more appropriately rendered as *"faithfulness"* in this passage.

Chapter 3:1-19   **Habakkuk's confidence in God**

*"I trembled inside when I heard all this; my lips quivered with fear. My legs gave way beneath me, and I shook with terror. I will <u>wait quietly</u> for the coming day when <u>disaster will strike the people who invade us</u>. Even though the fig trees have no blossoms, and there are no grapes on the vine; even though the olive crop fails, and the fields lie empty and barren; even though the flocks die in the fields, and the cattle barns are empty, <u>**yet I will rejoice in the Lord! I will be joyful in the God of my salvation. The Sovereign Lord is my strength!**</u>"* (vv. 16-19, NLT, emphasis mine).

What a powerful statement of confidence in the Almighty! Imagining the worst is coming (God's judgment for idol worship), he settles two vital issues in his own heart. (1) God knows what He is doing, so I will simply be patient in waiting for the eternal plan to unfold in His timing. (2) Because of this confidence, I will walk in faithfulness and rejoice in spite of the difficult circumstances.

Is this not akin to what Paul wrote to the Philippian church from prison in Rome? *"Rejoice in the Lord always: and again I say, Rejoice"* (Philippians 4:4). The premise for the Apostle's rejoicing was certainly not predicated on the quality of circumstances or even in the hope of significant change (while he was on earth). The resounding message is that true rejoicing transcends human circumstance and is confidently secured by our relationship with God in Christ Jesus (Philippians 4:11-13).

THE SOVEREIGN ONE IS PURPOSE-DRIVEN

Everything that God does has *purpose.* Many of the specific answers we seek are hidden to us, but the Sovereign God is never confused or frustrated. Briefly, we will discuss a few of the more obvious purposes that are visible to us through (1) Scripture, (2) relationship with Him, and (3) life experiences we encounter.

• To benefit Himself

Here is where many people, even believers, struggle. An erroneous concept depicts God as some cruel despot, always demanding that His subjects grovel in the dirt. Nothing is further from the truth. Actually, for many such a negative reaction toward God is an overt expression of pride and selfishness. God *owes* me. My *rights* have been violated. It is an evil attitude that has leeched itself into the minds of unbelievers. Unfortunately, some who profess Christ have been influenced by such foolish thinking.

Did God *need* to create man in order to be fulfilled? Absolutely not! His eternal purpose was to create a being who would voluntarily enter into the circle of fellowship enjoyed by the Father, Son, and Holy Spirit. And, when man sinned and broke this relational privilege, did God change His mind? Absolutely not! It was His unilateral decision to offer mercy and grace to the disobedient.

"Long ago, even before he made the world, God loved us and chose us to be holy and without fault in his eyes. His unchanging plan has always been to adopt us into his own family by bringing us to himself through Jesus Christ. And this gave him great pleasure" (Ephesians 1:4,5, NLT, emphasis mine). Read the entire book of Ephesians to discover the many times that Paul refers to this wonderful plan of redemption—which is *according* to God's purpose. (The word *according* is used 15 times in Ephesians.)

Now one will ask, "How does this benefit God?" The Amplified Version seems to express it most clearly and concisely. *"By having the eyes of your heart flooded with light, so that you can know and understand the hope to which He has called you and how rich is His glorious inheritance in the saints—His set-apart ones"* (Ephesians 1:18, Amp.). Literally, saints have become God's inheritance! It begs the question. What *benefits* do those who are His inheritance receive?

"The Spirit itself beareth witness with our spirit, that we are the children of God; and if children, then heirs; heirs of God, and joint-heirs with Christ" (Romans 8:16,17,

emphasis mine). The incomprehensible truth is that we are *fellow* heirs with Christ. The New Living Translations reads: *"Since we are his children, we will share his treasures—for everything God gives to his Son, Christ, is ours, too."* This does not describe a greedy, self-centered God. He is a kind, benevolent Father who has done and is doing everything for depraved man to become a part of His fellowship. Can we grasp such love? His personal reward is the redeemed sinful sons of Adam.

• To establish confidence

The Bible is filled with prophecies concerning various aspects of human life and history. There are scores of prophecies relating to **events, individuals, births, deaths, nations,** and **cities.** There are prophecies that **were fulfilled in Christ** and other prophecies **spoken by Christ.** One cannot correlate Scripture with human history without concluding that God has vindicated His own Word time after time. With each fulfilled prophecy the level of confidence that we have in this Sovereign Lord is ratcheted up to another level.

Of course, there are numerous prophecies that are yet to be fulfilled. These **end-time** prophecies speak of the **Rapture, Tribulation, Antichrist, Millennium** and the establishment of the **eternal kingdom.** The sequence of these events has been theological fodder for centuries. With each new dictator or political uprising another book will be written describing how God is going to culminate His future plan. This is not a critical remark, for every child of

God should be soberly and sincerely looking for the coming of the Lord. (Personally, I believe that Christ could come for His bride at any moment.) However, one must be careful to not get caught up in looking for "signs" rather than for the imminent return of the Lord.

While our view of the future is severely restricted, it is no stretch to conclude that God's plan is right on schedule. Why? Simple. He has repeatedly proven himself through the fulfillment of hundreds of prophecies as the One True God who keeps His word. With each passing day, the confidence that a believer has in the Almighty should increase.

"For ever, O Lord, thy word is settled in heaven" (Psalm 119:89).

"The grass withereth, the flower fadeth: but the word of our God shall stand forever" (Isaiah 40:8)

"Heaven and earth shall pass away, but my words shall not pass away" (Matthew 24:35)

• To benefit others

I am frequently amazed at how easily people can overlook this prominent purpose of God. The Word of God is not some depressing, outdated book of rules and regulations. It is relevant to every generation and every culture. By vigilantly pursuing its precepts heavenly blessings flow into our lives. Literally, they cannot be contained.

This is not fantasy. It is not hyper emotionalism or arrogant wishful thinking. In the Book of Deuteronomy (the final five sermons of Moses), he plainly articulates that the people of Israel have a choice—*obedience produces blessings from God* and *disobedience results in being cursed by God.* But, they had to consistently make the right choices. They could not expect to claim the blessings if they were disobedient or even half-hearted in their obedience.

*"**If** thou shalt <u>hearken diligently</u> unto the voice of the Lord thy God, <u>to observe and to do all his commandments</u>...all these <u>blessings shall come</u> on thee, and <u>overtake thee</u>, **if** thou shalt hearken unto the voice of the Lord thy God"* (Deuteronomy 28:1,2, emphasis mine). In the first 14 verses of this chapter, Moses enumerates *21 specific ways* in which they could anticipate God's blessings.

As a young boy, I was a bit overweight. Consequently, being short and chubby, I could never outrun anyone. One day many years later, while reading this passage, I was intrigued by this word *"overtake."* Suddenly I had a mental picture of my younger days, of desperately trying to outrun someone, but always being overtaken. It was a delightful moment when I realized that it is *utterly impossible to escape* the blessings of God when you walk in obedience. He will catch you!

"Trouble chases sinners, while blessings chase the righteous" (Proverbs 13:21, NLT).

LIVING FOR CHRIST...

PROVIDES FOR A *BETTER PRESENT*

AND PROMISES A *BETTER FUTURE.*

A well-worn excuse for not serving the Lord is that it is too difficult. There are simply too many things to give up. What foolish conjecture. Honestly, can anyone name even one thing that is worth having in life that God's children are required to give up? Everything from *disease* to *destitution* haunts those whose lives are controlled by sin.

"Fools, because of their transgression, and because of their iniquities, are afflicted" (Psalm 107:17).

"Good understanding giveth favor: but the way of transgressors is hard" (Proverbs 13:15).

Peter said to the Lord, *"We've given up everything to follow you. What will we get out of it?"* (Matthew 19:27, NLT).

Jesus responded, *"And everyone who has given up houses or brothers or sisters or father or mother or children or property, for my sake, will receive a hundred times as much in return and will have eternal life"* (Matthew 19:29, NLT, emphasis mine). Sadly, some people equate the blessings that Christ promised with money and other material possessions. Again, this cruelly distorts the nature of a loving God.

The old hymn, sung in an earlier era by people who had precious few of the costly goods of earth, speaks so eloquently.

"Count your blessings, name them one by one,
Count your blessings, see what God has done.
Count your blessings, name them one by one,
Count your many blessings, see what God has done."

It might be a profitable spiritual exercise to pause at this moment and attempt to count our blessings. (Hint: don't begin with "things" you own.)

• To reward obedience

Jesus taught about rewards. Remember the Parable of the Talents? To the man who had received five and gained five others, and the man who had received two and gained two others, the Lord had words of commendation. *"Well done, my good and faithful servant. You have been faithful in handling this small amount, so now I will give you many more responsibilities. Let's celebrate together!"* (Matthew 25:21, 23, NLT).

Here the word used is *"faithful"* implying that the men were *trustworthy.* However, it hardly seems possible to extract or eliminate the concept of *obedience* from the story. The master had instructed them to invest the money for him. The one servant who was punished did not invest the money—he was disobedient.

In this life there are glorious rewards for following Christ, but certainly none to compare with the day we stand in the presence of Almighty God and He personally welcomes us into His presence. It really will be *worth it all*!

• To punish disobedience

Man has been afforded a free will with the power to choose good or evil. God never intended for man to be banished from His eternal presence. That is a choice each individual must make. In a self-justifying defense, one may say, "God is too good to send anyone to hell. He is, after all, a God of love." To both statements a believer will quickly agree. The Sovereign One is not vindictive; His purpose is that not even one person suffer eternal punishment. Peter expresses this truth in speaking of the apparent delay in the coming judgment of God upon sinful men. *"The Lord does not delay and be tardy or slow about what He promises, according to some people's conception of slowness, but He is long-suffering (extraordinarily patient) toward you, not desiring that any should perish, but that all should turn to repentance"* (2 Peter 3:9, Amp.).

The plan of redemption was costly to God. Jesus Christ, the Son of God, alone could become our sin substitute. The theme of the entire Bible exposes the heart of God. *"For God so <u>loved the world,</u> that he <u>gave his only begotten Son,</u> that whosoever believeth in him <u>should not perish,</u> but have ever-lasting life. For <u>**God sent not his Son into the world to condemn the world**</u>; but that the world through him might be saved"* (John 3:16,17, emphasis mine). Ultimately, a just God who cannot tolerate sin, punishes those who reject Him.

MAKE NO MISTAKE—JESUS IS THE ONLY WAY

TO BE RECONCILED TO GOD

"There is none other name under heaven

given among men,

whereby we must be saved."

Acts 4:12

When you carefully examine the divine purpose that is (1) ***established in immutability***, (2) ***motivated by love***, and

(3) *sealed by sacrifice* every reason for doubt and fear dissolves in the vastness of His majesty.

With *deep reverence* and *willing submission* we bow in *humility* before our Sovereign God. With *thankful hearts* and *confident trust* we acknowledge His wise authority. From this very moment until He chooses for us to enter into eternal glory we rest in His loving favor.

CHAPTER FIVE

Introduce Your God

Years ago while serving as a state youth director, I was introduced one Sunday morning as DCAP Lednicky. (The acrostic stood for District Christ's Ambassadors President.) A gentlemen who only occasionally attended church was present that morning with his family. His daughter later related that on the way home from church, her dad had expressed sympathy for the speaker. She had asked, "Why?" His response was classic. "To have a last name like Lednicky is bad enough, but to have DCAP as a first name is awful. I wonder where his parents ever came up with such a name."

Introductions are important. What we say or do not say often portrays an image to listeners. That may be extremely good or equally bad. So, if you were requested to stand before a group of people to *introduce your God*, how would you respond? Can you think of several descriptive words and the definition you would employ?

Quite likely at the top of most lists would be *love, holiness,* and *truth*. These, like all divine attributes, do not fit into a ranking system. One is not greater nor lesser than the other as they are equally expressed in *absolute perfection*. These moral virtues are inherent in the very nature of God. Simply stated, love, holiness, and truth are first and foremost expressions of who He is, and then actively expressed toward His creation. It is crucial to our faith to have a working knowledge of how each defines the eternally existent God. Yet, our understanding must extend beyond the conceptual. The majestic truth of Scripture opens the window slightly for us to peek into the spirit world and discover how this great God interacts with individuals in a personal manner.

OLD TESTAMENT NAMES OF GOD

Elohim	*"God"*	Genesis 1:1
Adonai	*"Lord"*	Malachi 1:6
Jehovah	*"Divine Savior"*	Genesis 2:4
Jehovah-Maccaddeshem	*"Lord-sanctifier"*	Exodus 31:13
Jehovah-Rohi	*"Lord-shepherd"*	Psalm 23:1

Jehovah-Shammah	*"Lord-present"*	Ezekiel 48:35
Jehovah-Rapha	*"Lord-our healer"*	Exodus 16:26
Jehovah-Tsidkenu	*"Lord-our righteousness"*	Jeremiah 23:6
Jehovah-Jireh	*"Lord-provider"*	Genesis 22:13, 14
Jehovah-Nissi	*"Lord-our banner"*	Exodus 17:15
Jehovah-Shalom	*"Lord-peace"*	Judges 6:24
Jehovah-Sabbaoth	*"Lord of Hosts"*	Isaiah 6:1-3
El-Elyon	*"Most High God"*	Genesis 14:17-20; Isaiah 14:13,14
El-Roi	*"Strong one who sees"*	Genesis 16:12
El-Shaddai	*"God Almighty"*	Genesis 17:1; Psalm 91:1
El-Olam	*"Everlasting God"*	Isaiah 40:28-31

DEPEND ON THE WORD OF GOD

The most accurate information about God comes directly from the Word of God. If you really want to know who God is, it is essential that you know what His Word says.

Allow a brief moment to emphasize the importance of *knowing* and *believing* God's Word. With the advent of new "revelations" almost daily, the solid truth of the **inspired, infallible** Word has been perverted. Many sincere people are confused by the multitude of conflicting voices. However, the syncretistic (combination of various, often mutually opposed beliefs, into a new, variegated conglomerate which is marked by internal inconsistencies) approach to Christian truth today is appalling. This may be expressed under the guise of tolerance, advanced scholarship, or changing times. In my evaluation, the biggest culprit giving rise to such hodgepodge is personal preference—a system of belief in which I can feel comfortable and justified in my behavior.

The prophet Hosea addressed this issue during the era in which Israel had fallen into idol worship. They were in a process of what might be described as mix-and-match religious system. The Temple and true worship had become polluted beyond description, and certainly far beyond Jehovah's level of tolerance. Relaying the Lord's indictment against Israel, the prophet wrote, *"My people are destroyed for the lack of knowledge"* (Hosea 4:6). They had abandoned His Word and sin became rampant. It always has and always will.

It would be comforting to say that the New Testament church was different. Unfortunately, many fell into the same deep pit. In his final letter, Paul admonishes Timothy to cling tenaciously to God's Word. In his description of the *"last days,"* the apostle declares that there will be those who *"will act as if they are religious, but they will reject the power that could make them godly"* (2 Timothy 3:5, NLT).

Concluding that evil will flourish, Paul again urges Timothy to stay true to God's Word. *"But you must remain faithful to the things you have been taught. You have been taught the holy Scriptures from childhood, and they have given you the wisdom to receive the salvation that comes by trusting in Christ Jesus. <u>All scripture is inspired by God and is useful to teach us what is true and make us realize what is wrong in our lives. It straightens us out and teaches us to do what is right</u>"* (2 Timothy 3:14-16, NLT, emphasis mine).

Why is he so emphatic? *"For the time will come when they will not endure sound doctrine; but after their own lust shall they heap to themselves teachers, having itching ears; and they shall turn away their ears from the truth, and shall be turned into fables"* (2 Timothy 4:3). (I prefer the King James here.) The New Living Translation says, *"They will look for teachers who will tell them whatever they want to hear."*

In His prayer just prior to the Cross, Christ prayed for the disciples (and for us). *"Sanctify them—purify, conse-crate, separate them for Yourself, make them holy—by the Truth. <u>Your Word is Truth</u>"* (John 17:17, Amp., emphasis mine). As we seek to know God, there must be no vacilla-tion. ***Our God must be the God of the Bible!***

• God is love

The beloved apostle John (the only member of the original Twelve who died a natural death) speaks clearly of God's love. He states, *"God is love"* (1 John 4:8). Then he quickly proceeds to show us how this loving God manifested His nature to man. *"God showed how much he loved us by sending his only Son into the world so that we might have eternal life through him. <u>This is real love</u>. It is not that we loved God, but that he loved us and sent his Son as a sacrifice to take away our sins"* (1 John 4:9,10, NLT, emphasis mine).

> **God's love is not a mushy emotion. It is a rational and voluntary affection, which is established in perfect reason and deliberate choice.**

Again, we are reminded that God did not need man to be fulfilled. If emotion had been the controlling factor of His love, He surely would have abandoned (or destroyed) Adam and Eve when they sinned in the Garden of Eden. It was divine initiative that sent Christ to this earth to become our sin substitute. We bring nothing to the table except our total unworthiness.

Another aspect of divine love is *discipline*. This is often confusing to those who want only what they want, when they want it. *Love is not always accommodating and conciliatory*. Parents understand this concept very well. Children have to be taught. They will not automatically grow up into productive, well-mannered, morally pure adults. On occasion, when a young person has committed some violent crime, the weeping parent will say, "I just loved him too much to discipline him." Actually, the opposite is true. If the parent had genuinely loved, he/she would have exerted every conceivable energy to prevent such a tragedy from occurring.

God cares enough about us to avert self-destruction. That means we will not always have "our own way." In His love—if, and only if, we recognize His hand as that of a loving Protector—we are safe. The little chorus says it quite well.

"He careth for you,
He careth for you,
Through sunshine or shadow,
He careth for you."

Introduce your God with deep affection as the ultimate expression of perfect love.

• God is holiness

God is holy in that He, and He alone, is the *source* and *standard* for all that is right. He must be understood as the author of all principles for moral behavior. God is not under

He is righteous by nature and, as such, His holiness is in perfect agreement with His being and His will.

God excludes from himself anything and everything that is contrary to His nature.

the law, nor above the law; He *is* law. The distinguishing factor of God's law is that it is exclusively for our blessing and benefit. Our faith is not controlled by fear. *God is holy, not harsh*—and there is a major difference.

This subject of *holiness* is no ancillary theme with God. Did you know that the words *holy* and *holiness* are mentioned **more than 500 times** in Scripture (150 in Exodus and Leviticus; approximately 170 by the prophets; almost 200 in the New Testament)?

Early on in God's progressive revelation of himself to man, He identifies His own holiness. *"For I am the Lord your God: ye shall therefore be holy, <u>for I am holy</u>"* (Leviticus 11:44,45; 19:2; 20:7). In urging New Testament believers to live in purity, Peter quotes this verse from Leviticus (1 Peter 1:16). The prophet **Isaiah** provides a graphic portrayal of God's awesome holiness. In his vision, he *"saw the Lord...sitting on a lofty throne, and the train of his robe filled the Temple. Hovering around him were mighty seraphim, each with six wings. With two wings they covered their faces, with two they covered their feet, and with the remaining two they flew. In a great chorus they sang, <u>'Holy, holy, holy is the Lord Almighty! The whole earth is filled with his glory!'</u>"* (Isaiah 6:1-3, NLT, emphasis mine). What was the prophet's reaction? In comparison with God's holiness, he saw himself as a *"sinful man and a member of a sinful race"* (Isaiah 6:5, NLT).

Jesus, God in the flesh, lived out holiness here on earth. **Paul** confirms the *"sinlessness"* of Christ in explaining how we have been reconciled to God. *"For God made Christ,* *who never sinned, to be the offering for our sin, so that we could be made right with God through Christ"* (2 Corinthians 5:21, NLT, emphasis mine).

Peter quotes from Isaiah 53, *"Who did no sin, neither was guile found in his mouth"* (1 Peter 2:22, emphasis mine).

John encourages believers to live in purity as Christ is pure. *"And you know that Jesus came to take away our sins, for there is no sin in him"* (1 John 3:5, NLT, emphasis mine).

The **writer of Hebrews** also speaks of the worthiness of our heavenly High Priest. *"This High Priest of ours understands our weaknesses, for the faced all of the same temptations we do, yet he did not sin"* (Hebrews 4:15, NLT, emphasis mine).

In these days of vulgarity and moral bankruptcy, the holiness of Almighty God gleams in brilliant contrast. In fact, it brings condemnation on those whose lives carry the putrid odor of sin. According to Jesus, such people *"love darkness rather than light, because their deeds are evil"* (John 3:19).

To the children of God who have grown weary with the spiritual pollution that surrounds us, to come into His presence is a blessed treat. His holiness is not a threat. It is the moral compass for life by which we navigate through a world that would attempt to pull us into the garbage dump of evil.

Introduce your God as the Holy One who through mercy and grace has made it possible for us to enter into His sinless presence—something no human can do outside of the sacrifice of Jesus Christ for our sins.

• God is Truth

All truth among men has its foundation in the creator God. Many philosophical attempts to find God end up in a state of confusion because they start with man and try to spiral upward. This is futile. It is as foolish as trying to put the roof on a house before the foundation has been laid. God not only reveals truth and justly does that which is just and true; He is by nature Truth.

As with much of our understanding of God, man needs visual evidence to adequately grasp this concept. Hence, the revelation of God through Jesus. Remember the angelic proclamation to Joseph that His name is to be *"Emmanuel, which being interpreted is, God with us"* (Matthew 1:23, emphasis mine). The disciples, confused about what was happening, pleaded, *"Lord, show us the Father and we will be satisfied."* To this Jesus responded, *"Anyone who has seen me has seen the Father"* (John 14:8,9, NLT). Earlier, replying to the incessant badgering of the Jewish leaders, Jesus had plainly declared, *"The Father and I are one"* (John 10:30, NLT).

When Jesus said, *"I am the way, the truth, and the life"* (John 14:6, emphasis mine), He was not simply confirming his truthfulness in relational matters. The inference was much deeper. More literally it could be translated, "I am He who is truth and the source of truth."

It is of equal significance to note that God the Spirit is identified by Christ as the *"Spirit of Truth"* (John 14:17; 15:26; 16:13) in the final teaching discourse He had with the disciples (as recorded in John 12-16) just prior to the Cross. There can be no question—the Holy Trinity is co-equal and co-glorious, equal in essence, substance, and power.

A word commonly used among us today is *integrity*. The corporate world suffers great loss when there is a perceived lack of integrity. Governmental powers are held up for ridicule when deliberate falsehoods are perpetrated. Homes are destroyed when marriage partners violate the bond of trust. In every aspect of society, honesty and integrity are indispensable. If this principle be true (no pun intended) among men, how much more does God understand it?

Balaam, the prophet who was tempted to compromise his message from God for the sake of more money, ultimately made a most profound confession. *"God is not a man, that he should lie. He is not a human, that he should change his mind. Has he ever spoken and failed to act? Has he ever promised and not carried it through?"* (Numbers 23:19, NLT). Those two rhetorical questions are quite easily answered with an unqualified no.

The Psalmist emphasizes the veracity of God in Psalm 119. Incidentally, this is the longest chapter in the Bible and all 176 verses speak about the *"statues"* or *"law"* of God. *"Thy word is true from the beginning: and everyone of thy righteous judgments endureth for ever"* (v. 160, emphasis mine).

65

With no doublespeak or spin on the truth, you can boldly introduce your God as the God who is Truth, and from whom all that is truth, true, and truthful emanates.

• The list is long

In such a short treatise, it is impossible to even identify the many qualities and attributes of the Almighty. Your personal list might include **goodness, mercy, grace, patience, justice,** and **righteous.** The one other aspect of God's character that simply cannot be omitted here is **faithfulness.** As Isaiah looks beyond the current circumstances of rebellious Israel, he extols the faithfulness of God. *"O Lord, you are my God; I will exalt and praise your name, <u>for in perfect faithfulness</u> you have done marvelous things, things planned long ago"* (Isaiah 25:1, NIV, emphasis mine). The phrase *"perfect faithfulness"* literally means faithfulness of reliability.

"Understand, therefore, that the Lord your God is indeed God. He is the <u>faithful God who keeps his covenant for a thousand generations</u>" (Deuteronomy 7:9, NLT, emphasis mine).

"I will declare that your love stands firm forever, that you <u>established your faithfulness</u> in heaven itself" (Psalms 89:2, NIV, emphasis mine).

"If we are faithless (do not believe and are untrue to Him), He remains true [<u>faithful to His Word and His righteous character</u>], for He cannot deny Himself" (2 Timothy 2:13, Amp., emphasis mine).

• **Never doubt it—God is true to His own Word**

Finally, the dimension of Deity that encompasses all these glorious attributes and holds them in harmonious balance—God is **perfect**.

> **HOLINESS WITHOUT LOVE IS HARSHNESS;**
> **LOVE WITHOUT HOLINESS IS COMPROMISE.**

Just prior to his death, Moses presented a majestic song to the assembly of all Israel. (It is recorded in its entirety in Deuteronomy 32:1-43.) One stanza says, *"He is the Rock; his work is perfect. Everything he does is just and fair. He is a faithful God who does not wrong; how just and upright he is!"* (Deuteronomy 32:4, NLT, emphasis mine).

"As for God, his way is perfect. All the Lord's promises prove true" (Psalm 18:30, NLT, emphasis mine).

Living in *constant imperfection*, the human mind struggles to grasp *constant perfection*. But that is our God—absolutely, irrevocably, infinitely, eternally perfect.

In this abbreviated study, I have personally come to a new dimension of *reverence, respect,* and *appreciation* for this great God we love and serve. But you may be asking, "What does this have to do with the subject of faith?" My response would be, "Everything!" Unless and until we know who our God is, at best, our faith is limited. Studying and learning His Word does not diminish faith; it dramatically increases it.

Coming to know Him will release your faith—confidence in His omnipotent power and trust in His omniscient wisdom.

O God, Our Help In Ages Past

O God, our help in ages past, Our hope for years to come, Our shelter from the stormy blast, and our eternal home!

Under the shadow of Thy throne Still may we dwell secure; Sufficient is Thine arm alone, and our defense is sure.

Before the hills in order stood, Or earth received her frame, From everlasting Thou art God, To endless years the same.

O God, our help in ages past, Our hope for years to come; Be Thou my guide while life shall last, And our eternal home.

—Isaac Watts

CHAPTER SIX

Reality Check

I stood waiting in the hospital hallway with the husband and son of a godly saint who was dying with cancer. The doctor solemnly walked out of the room and quietly said, "She is gone." The son, far away from his Christian upbringing, went into a rage, beat his fists against the wall, and snarled, "If this is how God treats His children, then I want nothing to do with Him."

While his pain at the death of his parent is understandable, his conclusion about God is fallacious. The fact is that this dear saint was not being *punished*, she was being *promoted*. Her exams were completed; she graduated from the temporal to the eternal.

Still we are prone to ask why there is all the pain and turmoil here on earth. The first truth to be established is that God is **not** the author or originator of evil. ***God is a good God—all the time.***

Second, we should be reminded why man was created. In the perfection and completeness of the Blessed Trinity, the Eternal One created man to participate in His love and fellowship. God did not need man, as we often "need" the affection and approval of another. He made himself available for man to share in the indescribable blessing and benefit of eternal glory.

Third, man was given a free will—that is, the power to choose. None of God's moral creation (angels or man) were to be forced into worship or service. The Almighty did not desire slaves. It is at this point that we can realistically embark upon a journey to discover why evil haunts our world and how it affects even the most godly.

• Man is depraved—really depraved

No litany of evil is required to prove this point. Watch the news for a week. You will be informed of one horrendous act after another. Road rage murder. Rape and incest. Fraud and cover-up into the hundreds of millions of dollars. Greed. Passion. Anger. Immorality to the degree that decent persons become sick just thinking about it.

This concept of depravity is not a contemporary idea. Long ago, the Word of God spoke directly to the universality of sin and wickedness.

"God looks down from heaven on the entire human race; he looks to see if there is even one with real understanding, one who seeks after God. But no, all have turned away from God; all have become corrupt. No one does

good, not even one!" (Psalm 53:2,3, NLT).

"All we like sheep have gone astray; we have turned everyone to his own way" (Isaiah 53:6).

"We are all infected and impure with sin. When we proudly display our righteous deeds, we find they are but filthy rags" (Isaiah 64:6, NLT).

"For all have sinned and come short of the glory of God" (Romans 3:23).

"You used to be just like the rest of the world, full of sin, obeying Satan...All of us used to live that way, following the passions and desires of our <u>evil nature</u>. <u>We were born with an evil nature</u>..." (Ephesians 2:2,3, NLT, emphasis mine).

If we say we have no sin, we are only fooling ourselves and refusing to accept the truth. If we claim we have not sinned, we are calling God a liar..." (1 John 1:8, 10, NLT).

The minds of great theologians have pondered whether man is a sinner because of Adam or because of his own sin. To me, the answer is obvious. It is not an either-or, it is an and-both. I have a *nature* (because of Adam's sin) that is bent toward evil, but I am also guilty because of *personal sin.* No passing the buck. Adam is not a convenient scapegoat. I am culpable and accountable for my own choices. There can only be one conclusion: sin is rampant as a result of man's total depravity. Only Christ can offer a cure.

• **Consequences of sin**

Two well-known Bible characters suffered dramatic

consequences for their sin. **David**, the sweet singer of Israel, man after God's own heart, committed adultery and murder. He repented, genuinely so. Psalm 51 reveals the deep contrition of his heart. But the rest of the record documents a string of events that are heartbreaking. The baby conceived out of the illicit affair died. One son, Amnon, raped his half-sister, Tamar. The more charismatic son, Absalom, precipitated an insurrection and David was forced to flee from the palace. His sin, like any sin, was costly.

The Nazarite **Samson**, strong man, mortal enemy of the Philistines, embarrassed them over and over again. Then one day he fell into their trap. Delilah cut his hair. His supernatural strength was gone. Now blind, his eyes gouged out, chained with fetters, day after day he ground at the millstone. In the end God restored his strength and he killed a throng of Philistines in the temple of their god Dagon.

> **God is merciful, but sin has a terribly large price tag.**
>
> **The Word of God is true—**
> *you will reap what you sow.*

Someone quickly counters, "But why must I suffer from another's wrongdoing? It doesn't seem quite fair." Sadly, there are times when believers bear the pain of sins for which they carry no guilt. From the human perspective it does come across as unjust. Natural disasters, war, economic collapse, prejudice, mistreatment by governments, abuse by employers, family tragedies, affect even the choicest of saints. In one portion of the Sermon on the Mount Jesus addresses the matter of loving those who are hateful and abusive. In this particular context He alludes to the matter of providence. *"For he [God] gives his sunlight to both the evil and the good, and he sends rain on the just and on the unjust, too"* (Matthew 5:45, NLT, explanation mine).

I love the Psalms for they allow us to hear human emotion being vented—often in raw fashion. One such expression is found in Psalm 73 (NLT). Asaph's frustration is obvious. *"But as for me, I came so close to the edge of the cliff! My feet were slipping, and I was almost gone. For I envied the proud when I saw them <u>prosper despite their wickedness</u>"* (vv. 2,3, emphasis mine). *"<u>These fat cats</u> have everything their hearts could ever wish for!* (v. 7, emphasis mine).

Listen to the pathos in his voice. *"<u>Was it for nothing</u> that I <u>kept my heart pure</u> and <u>kept myself from doing wrong</u>? <u>All I get is trouble</u> all day long; every morning brings me pain"* (vv. 13,14, emphasis mine). *"So I tried to understand why the wicked prosper. But what a difficult task it is!* (v. 16).

Finally, the psalmist opens his heart to God in the sanctuary and realizes the ultimate end of such people. He also confesses to his own wrong attitudes. *"Then I realized how bitter I had become, how pained I had been by all that I had seen. I was so foolish and ignorant..."* (vv. 21,22). His realigned spiritual view? *"Whom have I in heaven but you? I desire you more than anything on earth"* (v. 25). *But as for me, how good it is to be near God! I have made the Sovereign Lord my shelter"* (v. 28).

Hold on, dear saint. God has the record book—and it is always correct. *"Weeping may endure for a night, but joy cometh in the morning"* (Psalm 30:5).

• Bad choices

I knew a young man who was diagnosed with sugar diabetes, but could control it with a careful diet. Instead, he constantly gorged himself on pies, candy, cakes, soft drinks (not diet), in spite of warning after warning from the physician. Needless to say, he died at an early age. He could possibly have had many more healthy, productive years. There can be little question. He suffered as a result of his own bad choices. This example is by no means an isolated event. The child of God should do everything to maintain his/her body as the temple of God.

A rather extensive list could be compiled of commonly noticed foolish choices. Relationships built on physical attraction often lead to deep emotional pain, to say nothing of the possibility of some form of sexually transmitted disease. Greed leads good businessmen down a pathway of dishonesty and ruthless violation of others. Teenagers, pressured by their peers, take that first drink or smoke a joint, and find themselves on a pathway leading to unacceptable behavior or even committing violent crimes.

Such can describe the culture of this generation. Sadly, many of these same bad choices (sins) are found among those who claim to be followers of Christ. How tragic! Parents who profess one thing, but live another at home wonder how and why their sons and daughters rebel against God.

Often it is more difficult for a young person who has lived under a bad example of Christianity to follow Christ than it is for a young person who has been in an environment where there is no pretense of a profession of faith.

God's moral plan for man is not a penalty. Everything that He has instructed us to do or not to do is for our benefit. This all-wise Father knows what is best for us. So, even if a person did not accept Jesus Christ as God's Son but obeyed the teaching of Scripture, his life would be far better than his unbelieving counterpart. Lest there be any misunderstanding, I am not suggesting that merely applying the principles of the Bible to one's daily activities is an adequate replacement for faith in Christ. The **only way** to eternal life is by repentance of sin and faith in the propitious sacrifice of Christ on the cross.

Good works and good choices alone will never open the door to eternal life.

The faith approach is to petition the Lord to help you with your choices, never blame Him for the undesirable consequences of your bad ones.

• Hostile environment

For some time I have been emphasizing that *there is no such thing as nonoffensive Christianity.* This conflict is not the outgrowth of some immature personality clash, philosophical difference, or cultural barrier. This is **God versus Satan**. It must be quickly added that God and Satan are not opposite equals. Lucifer (the devil) was at one time among the highest ranking angels, but pride filled his mind and he sought to overthrow the Throne of God. He was banished from heaven (one-third of the angels fell with him) and allowed a season of time before his ultimate damnation.

"A final word: Be strong with the Lord's mighty power. Put on all of God's armor so that you will be able to stand firm against all the strategies and tricks of the Devil. <u>For we are not fighting against people made of flesh and blood</u>, but against the <u>evil rulers and authorities of the unseen world</u>, against those <u>mighty powers of darkness</u> who rule this world, and against the <u>wicked spirits in the heavenly realms</u>. Use every piece of God's armor to resist the enemy in the time of evil, so that after the battle you will be standing firm" (Ephesians 6:10-13, NLT, emphasis mine).

"For though we walk [live] in the flesh, we are not carrying on our warfare according to the flesh and using mere human weapons. For the weapons of our warfare are not physical (weapons of flesh and blood), but they are mighty before God for the overthrow and destruction of strongholds, [Inasmuch as we] refute arguments and theories and reasonings and every proud and lofty thing

that sets itself up against the (true) knowledge of God" (2 Corinthians 10:3-5, Amp.).

In his masterful comparison of the believer to a soldier prepared to engage in war, the apostle Paul outlines each piece of armor to be worn (Ephesians 6:14-18). All are vital; however, for our purposes here let's identify only two pieces. In my opinion, they are by far the most significant. If you lose or fail to make appropriate use of either when engaged in spiritual warfare, certain disaster is imminent. They are: **the shield of faith** and the **sword of the Spirit**. The first is *defensive*; the latter is *offensive.* The scriptural record provides this insight. *"Above all, taking the shield of faith, wherewith ye shall be able to quench all the fiery darts of the wicked"* (v. 16). The New Living Translation phrases it: *"In every battle you will need <u>faith as your shield</u> to <u>stop the fiery arrows aimed at you by Satan"</u>* (emphasis mine).

Simply, *"the sword of the Spirit"* is defined *"which is the word of God."* In this hostile environment, it is not deep conviction or a courageous heart that will defeat the enemy, as significant as these may be. Our Commander-in-chief has supplied us with the superior firepower—the Word of God.

> *IF JESUS COULD DEFEAT SATAN WITH THREE VERSES FROM THE BOOK OF DEUTERONOMY, SURELY WE CAN OVERCOME HIM WITH THE ENTIRE WORD OF GOD.*

Often we tend to look at the *"giants in the land"* rather than at the covenant promises of God. Yes, there are battles—difficult, heart-wrenching, emotionally fatiguing battles. This is not to deny the reality of the enemy, rather to point to the source of victory.

John so eloquently speaks of how the saint defeats the *"spirit of antichrist"* which is *"even now already in the world"* (1 John 4:3). *"Ye are of God, little children, and have overcome them: because <u>greater is he that is in you, than he that is in the world</u>"* (1 John 4:4, emphasis mine). He further amplifies this message later in this same epistle. *"For whatsoever is born of God overcometh the world: and <u>this is the victory that overcometh the world, even our faith</u>"* (1 John 5:4, emphasis mine).

In Romans 8, Paul asked two strategic questions. *"If God be for us, who can be against us?"* One translation says, *"If God is for us, what difference does it make who is against us?"* Then he posed a second rhetorical question. *"Who shall separate us from the love of Christ?"* After an elaborate list of those things which cannot separate us from our Lord, he declares, *"In all these things we are <u>more than conquerors through him who loved us</u>"* (Romans 8: 31-39, emphasis mine).

• Basic Training

This is the tough part. Tests that come straight from God. And to further complicate the issue, we do not always know which ones they are. Is the devil attacking or is God stretching us to another level of faith? Have you ever sung the chorus *"To be like Jesus—all I ask is to be like Him"* and then fret and wonder where God is when He begins to answer that petition? Our Heavenly Father knows exactly how mature we are spiritually. It is His desire, far more than ours, to move the liabilities of our lives into the asset column.

> **He has not planned failure for your life.**
> **However, in the process of progressing from Point A**
> **to Point B spiritually, there will be divinely**
> **ordered obstacle courses.**

Do you recall your parents "requiring" you to wash your hands before meals or take a bath at night? If you are male, you probably do. Now, you smile and wonder why that ever seemed to be such a difficult chore. It's a no-brainer. Today, it is pleasantly refreshing and extremely healthy. As a believer you quickly grasp the analogy. Certain aspects of the faith walk seemed so demanding and unnecessary. Yet, God kept on insisting. Trials and tests came with regularity until one day the light came on. You understood that a loving Father was longing only to keep you from the injury of dangerous pitfalls. He knew what was ahead—and He cared.

> **God loves His children too much to allow them**
> **to self-destruct without doing everything possible**
> **to prevent it from happening.**

The writer of Hebrews approaches this subject in such a positive manner. *"And have you entirely forgotten the <u>encouraging words</u> God spoke to you, his children? He said, 'My child, don't ignore it when the Lord disciplines you, and don't be discouraged when he corrects you. For the <u>Lord disciplines those he loves,</u> and he punishes those he accepts as his children.' As you endure this <u>divine discipline</u>, remember that <u>God is treating you as his own children.</u>*

"But God's discipline is <u>always right and good for us</u> because it means we will share in his holiness. No discipline is enjoyable while it is happening—it is painful! But afterward there will be a <u>quiet harvest of right living</u> for those who are trained in this way" (Hebrews 12:5-7,10,11, NLT, emphasis mine).

Children are seldom impressed when a parent says, "This hurts me worse than it hurts you." Have you ever had the same attitude toward God? If so, it may be one indication that your faith needs more training. Basic training does not teach you everything. It is not the ultimate goal. No true soldier expects to receive an honorable discharge upon the completion of a few weeks of basic training. All the strenuous exercise, all the discomfort, all the demands are preparatory. This only qualifies the recruit to be tested in greater dimension in actual battle situations.

So, here we are stuck right in the big middle of a sin sick world. Jesus identified this place as *"the gates of Hell."* For a season Satan is called the *"god of this world."* And, it often seems that he is surely in control. Bad things happen as he vomits out his poison on mankind. It is a sad, sad picture if you are locked into this distorted view.

> **What you are doing today is as significant as what you will be doing 20 years from now. Today is forming within you the tenacity and strength to meet the challenges of your tomorrow. You will not be ready to meet contingencies of the future until you have successfully completed and passed the test of today.**

For the believer there is a bright, eternal dimension— **Jesus is building His church, just as He promised!** And, in the end, *"every knee will bow...and every tongue confess that Jesus Christ is Lord to the glory of God the Father"* (Philippians 3:10,11).

Dear faithful saint, grasp your faith firmly. Wrap yourself securely in it. The ride may be bumpy for a while. Never allow fear to control your thoughts. It is all going to be OK. *God will keep His Word—eternity will prove it.*

"Living by faith in Jesus above,
Trusting, confiding in His great love.
From all harm safe, in His sheltering arms,
I'm living by faith, and I feel no alarm."

CHAPTER SEVEN

Level **Five** *Faith*

The development of faith is a process. It does not mature instantly. Time, experience, understanding of scriptural truth, prayer, spiritual discipline, and other components are ingredients in this lifelong journey.

FIVE LEVELS OF FAITH

1. *SAVING*
2. *SANCTIFYING*
3. *SUPERNATURAL*
4. *SUFFERING*
5. *SUBMISSIVE*

As a compass to guide us in our search for understanding and, subsequently, application of this most complex of biblical truth, I have identified *five levels* in the development of mature faith. To be sure, there are no exact boundary lines in crossing from one level to the next. Nor must one assume that each is mutually exclusive from the others. What can be stated with certainty is that one *must begin* with level one—*saving faith.* The ultimate desire of every child of God should be to strive for level five—*submissive faith.*

The pathway between these two points will be individually discovered. No standardized tests. In His infinite wisdom, God has planned a course that is uniquely designed for our *faith development.* As we proceed in our discussion of these checkpoints, perhaps you can evaluate your progress. There may be some strong and some weaker areas. Allow the Spirit to be your proctor. You can be confident that He will give you an honest and fair grade!

LEVEL ONE—*SAVING FAITH*

For the natural mind it is a leap too wide to risk. The Virgin Birth? The Cross and Resurrection? Simple confession of sin and total forgiveness? Human reason and intellect alone simply cannot grasp God's merciful plan of redemption. The eternal dimension of the sacrifice of Christ comes only by divine revelation—and that requires faith.

The Philippian jailer asked the most significant question ever posed by fallen mankind, *"Sirs, what must I do to be saved?"* The answer that Paul and Silas gave profoundly sums up the message of the gospel in one succinct sentence.

"Believe on the Lord Jesus and you will be saved, along with your entire household" (Acts 16:30,31, NLT).

• The intellect is involved

"So then faith cometh by hearing, and hearing by the word of God" (Romans 10:17). It is at this initial entry point that most people hesitate. They do not embrace the authority of Scripture. Especially in a postmodern culture is this true. The argument goes something like this, "The Word of God may be your truth, but it is not mine." After ministering in a number of nations where the principles of the Bible have never been taught, I realize more and more the depravity of man's mind. ***The seed of faith must begin to grow before one can truly "hear" the Word of God.***

• A public response is required

"That if thou shalt <u>confess with thy mouth</u> the Lord Jesus, and shall <u>believe in thine heart</u> that God hath raised him from the dead, thou shalt be saved. For with the heart man believeth unto righteousness; and <u>with the mouth confession is made unto salvation</u>" (Romans 10:9,10, emphasis mine). Faith (believe in your heart) and confession are inextricably linked. If you believe, you will confess. However, it is possible to say that you believe, without really doing so. Incidentally, the Greek word for confess, *homologeo,* is stronger than mental assent. It is being together in covenant. That is, the heart and the mouth are one. This is the same word that Christ used when He was instructing the disciples for their first preaching mission.

"Whosoever therefore shall <u>confess</u> me before men, him will I also <u>confess</u> before my Father which is in heaven" (Matthew 10:32, emphasis mine).

• Man's relationship with God is restored

"Therefore being <u>justified by faith</u>, we have peace with God through our Lord Jesus Christ" (Romans 5:1, emphasis mine). It seems incredulous that any human—created in the very image of God—would blatantly reject this unilateral offer for forgiveness and restoration. In his persuasive letter to the believers at Ephesus, Paul contrasts the sinful state of man with the mercy and grace of God. His conclusion? *"For by grace are ye <u>saved through faith</u>: and that not of yourselves: it is the gift of God: not of works, lest any man should boast"* (Ephesians 2:8,9, emphasis mine).

Why is this so difficult? It is much, much more than the stubbornness of human intellect. This is Satan's first line of defense. It goes all the way back to the Garden of Eden. *"Hath God said"* was intended to deposit a seed of doubt into Eve's mind. Although Adam and Eve disobeyed—and we, the sons and daughters of the *"first Adam,"* are also guilty—God countered the lies of the enemy. Jesus, the very Son of God, took the punishment of our sins to the cross. The glorious covenant was confirmed at His resurrection. And, in order to be restored to a place of fellowship with the Almighty, all I have to do is believe that God's plan is for real. As a born-again believer, why not take a few moments to lay this book aside and give thanks and rejoice in your salvation.

LEVEL TWO—*SANCTIFYING FAITH*

Wandering in the wilderness was never God's plan for the Children of Israel. After the miraculous deliverance from Egyptian bondage and the subsequent crossing of the Red Sea, the Jewish people were finally free. Now they could claim the "promised land." But here they balked. Listening to the report of the ten spies, they grew fearful and even wanted to return to slavery. It seems so irrational. How quickly they forgot what God had just done for them after more than 400 years in Egypt.

According to Scripture, what should have been a few days journey lasted 40 years—going around in circles. *"Normally it takes only eleven days to travel from Mount Sinai to Kadesh- barnea, going by way of Mount Seir. But forty years after the Israelites left Mount Sinai..."* (Deuteronomy 1:2,3, NLT). (Kadesh-barnea was the site of the first crossing into the Promised Land.)

There were some miracles in the wilderness. The manna, the supply of water from the rock, the clothes that did not wear out were evidences that God was with them. Yet, all those who were 20 years of age or older when they left Egypt died in the wilderness. Why? ***They did not have faith to enter into the full blessings of God's promise.***

This historical event of Old Testament record is frequently noted as a reference point in the New Testament. The application for present-day believers is easily recognized. ***The experience of salvation is only the beginning point in faith development.*** The new birth is exactly that. As a child begins to grow, he/she develops motor skills, comprehends words and concepts, and, in the course of time with proper training, makes a contribution to society.

Although the apostle Paul commended the Corinthians as having *"every spiritual gift you need"* (1 Corinthians 1:7, NLT), he also reprimanded them for spiritual immaturity. *"Dear brothers and sisters, when I was with you I couldn't talk to you as I would to mature Christians. I had to talk as though you belonged to this world or as though you were infants in the Christian life. I had to feed you with milk and not with solid food, because you couldn't handle anything stronger. And you still aren't ready, for you are still controlled by your own sinful desires"* (1 Corinthians 3:1-3, NLT).

The desire of the Lord Jesus is to bring every believer to spiritual maturity, so that his life will be a reflection of God's grace and glory (2 Corinthians 3:18).

Often the Pharisees are held up as examples—usually in a negative light. Of course, Jesus was in constant conflict with them and used some strong language in exposing the hypocrisy of their hearts. But let's look at the other side for a moment. Early on, this group of religious leaders had been known as "separatists" for their unwavering adherence to the Law of Moses. Unfortunately, along the way somewhere they became "elitists." In our understanding of *sanctification*, they met the first half. The Pharisees were *set apart from*. You will recall that Jesus did not criticize them for their very strict observance of external matters of the Law. However, these religious leaders are evidence that such conformation alone does not fulfill the scriptural definition of sanctification.

The Bible does, in fact, teach that we are to be *set apart from* the overt sins of this world. In both Ephesians and Colossians Paul urges these converts to *"put off the old man"* and *"put on the new man"* (Ephesians 4:22-24; Colossians 3:8-14). In his letter to the Galatians he admonishes, *"So I advise you to live according to your new life in the Holy Spirit. Then you won't be doing what your sinful nature craves. The old sinful nature loves to do evil, which is just opposite from what the Holy Spirit wants"* (Galatians 5:16,17, NLT). Then, spelling it out very explicitly, he **identifies 17 sins of the flesh** from which believers are to be separated (Galatians 5:19-21). After enumerating the *fruit of the Spirit*, he provides a brief summation. *"Those who belong to Christ Jesus have nailed the passions and desires of their sinful nature to his cross and crucified them there"* (Galatians 5:24, NLT).

It is possible to follow a dogma or creed and fulfill one's obligation to a church organization. It is even possible to refrain from doing all the things that are listed as overt sins in Scripture. Please understand. This is right and good. As the sons and daughters of the Most High God, we are to live in a manner that is befitting our "family name." However, that is only one aspect of sanctification.

SANCTIFICATION
To be set apart FROM
and
To be set apart UNTO
Scriptural sanctification requires both

The truth is that most will not be *set apart from* for a lifetime unless they have also been *set apart unto*. In the dissertation of the True Vine (John 15), Jesus addresses the heart of the matter. He repeatedly encourages the disciples to *"abide in me."* (He uses the word *abide* eight times in this one chapter.) This is understandable. There is no spiritual life outside of belonging to Christ. But, here the Lord takes it a step further. His explanation erases any confusion about the *set apart unto* side of sanctification. *"Ye have not chosen me, but I have chosen you, and ordained you, that ye should go and bring forth fruit, and that your fruit should remain"* (John 15:16).

This is the major test of the faith-sanctification process. What I am <u>willing not to do</u> is vital, but of equal (if not greater) significance is what I am <u>willing to do</u>. Some achieve a level of great spiritual discipline, abandoning the lifestyle of unbelievers. Yet, those same individuals are stubbornly unwilling to make a full and total surrender to the claims of Christ. Frustration is inevitable. You can't have it both ways. Turning away from without turning to creates a vacuum. Victorious spiritual life does not exist in such a place.

For most of us it became obvious soon after our conversion. "I can't do this," we often thought. Perhaps we were quick to remind the Lord of our weaknesses and inabilities. We wept with each failure and even considered giving up. Herein lies both the problem and the answer. The problem—I can't. The answer—He can.

So how have saints of 50 or 60 years' duration managed to walk in victory? By faith, they claimed the promises of God and crossed the Jordan into the Land of Promise. There were giants of temptation, evil all around, but they chose to look beyond what the natural eye could see and envision what was ahead. By faith, they have allowed the Holy Spirit to work within, fashioning the image of Christ day by day. The faith necessary to establish a right relationship with God will also serve well in maintaining and enriching that relationship.

LEVEL THREE—*SUPERNATURAL FAITH*

At this point, we come loaded with a notebook full of questions. "Why does God heal some and not others?" would probably rank near the top of most lists. "Does the answer always come according to our desires, if we have faith?" "How can I know the difference between faith and presumption or emotion?" "Is it unscriptural to keep on praying for a specific need if the answer does not come immediately?"

There will always be many unanswered questions concerning the miraculous and its relationship to our faith. Some cannot be answered, simply because God alone knows (1) what is in His plan and (2) what is in our hearts. As we search to more fully develop our faith, let's begin with the foundation. ***The supernatural manifestation of God's power in response to our petitions will not occur without faith.***

• An Indispensable Objective—God's Glory

You can't miss it in the words of Jesus. Everything He did was to glorify His Father. He clearly articulated that consequential message to the disciples. Listen to His instructions.

> *"He that believeth on me, the works that I do shall he do also; and greater works than these shall he do; because I go unto my Father. And whatsoever ye shall ask in my name, that will I do, <u>that the Father may be glorified in the Son</u>. If ye shall ask anything in my name, I will do it"* (John 14:12-14, emphasis mine).

> *"If ye abide in me, and <u>my words abide in you</u>, ye shall ask what ye will, and it shall be done unto you"* (John 15:7, emphasis mine).

John the Beloved trumpeted this same directive. *"And whatsoever we ask, we receive of him, because we <u>keep his commandments</u>, and do those things that are <u>pleasing in his sight</u>"* (1 John 3:22, emphasis mine).

> *"And this is the confidence that we have in him, that, if we <u>ask anything according to his will</u>, he heareth us: And, if we know that he hear us, whatsoever we ask, we know that we have the petitions that we desired of him"* (1 John 5:14,15, emphasis mine).

No superstars. No one-up-manship. Simple faith, humbly expressed by an obedient believer, in harmony with His will moves the hand of the Almighty.

• Divine Healing is included in the Atonement

The Psalmist blesses the Lord and remembers *"all his benefits: Who forgiveth all thine iniquities; <u>who healeth all thy diseases;</u>"* (Psalm 103:3, emphasis mine).

Isaiah, the Messianic prophet, portrays the sufferings of Christ as being both substitutionary and efficacious for sin and sickness. In the well-known Chapter 53, he poetically describes the Atonement. *"But he was wounded for our transgressions, he was bruised for our iniquities: the chastisement of our peace was upon him; <u>and with his stripes we are healed</u>"* (Isaiah 53:5, emphasis mine).

In his first epistle, Peter points to the suffering of Christ and pictures Him as the sinless Savior. *"Who his own self bare our sins in his body on the tree, that we, being dead to sins, should live unto righteousness: <u>by whose stripes ye were healed</u>"* (1 Peter 2:24, emphasis mine).

Now we are faced with an interesting question. If physical healing was paid for on the Cross, just as were our sins, then why are not all believers healed? Remember that we previously discussed the complete process of redemption. The curse of death is the *"last enemy to be destroyed"* [rendered of none effect, useless] (1 Corinthians 15:26).

> *Death was <u>defeated</u> by the cross*
> *and resurrection of Christ,*
> *but it will be <u>destroyed</u> in the future*
> *at the resurrection of the saints.*

Paul reminds us that the *"whole creation groaneth and travaileth in pain until now. And not only they, but ourselves also, which have the firstfruits of the Spirit, even we ourselves groan within ourselves, <u>waiting for the adoption, to wit, the redemption of our body</u>"* (Romans 8:22,23. emphasis mine).

Does this mean that we cease praying for the sick, since, after all, sooner or later we will all die (unless the rapture of the Church occurs in our lifetime)? Absolutely not. It is always in accordance with Scripture to continually petition the Lord for a miracle of healing. As finite beings, our view into His *timing* is obscured. In extraordinary situations, the Lord may reveal His plan for one's future health. The appropriate response is always complete submission, in faith accepting His word, and being emotionally composed with peace of mind and spirit.

• Who has the faith?

Is the person who is ill responsible to have faith for the supernatural? Or, do the elders (believers) who are called upon to pray bear the weight of exercising faith? Or, could it be that the individual who brought the sick person to be prayed for had the faith that moved God to action? Of course, this is foolish speculation. Only the omniscient God could possibly have this kind of communication with His creation. In my opinion, the best case scenario would be that all persons involved were acting in faith—in obedience to the Word of God.

James outlines the pattern. *"Is any one of you sick? He should call the elders of the church to pray over him and anoint him with oil in the name of the Lord. And the prayer offered in faith will make the sick person well; the Lord will raise him up"* (James 5:14,15, NIV, emphasis mine). Incidentally, the term *"elder"* refers to spiritual maturity rather than a leadership (pastoral) role in the church.

> *The principal consideration should not be who has the faith, rather that it is the Lord Jesus who is the healer.*

One night I was speaking for a pastors conference, the Holy Spirit prompted my heart to ask those who had a specific need for a miraculous healing to come to the platform. Several came forward to be prayed for that evening. Approximately one year later in a different location, a pastor that I had previously never met approached me after the service. He told me that he had been in the pastors conference and had been suffering with a serious heart ailment for almost two years. He could not drive and often was unable to fill the pulpit on Sunday morning. That night he came to the platform "believing that God had spoken" and "this was to be his night for healing." He excitedly told me that he drove home that night and had been driving ever since. Without suffering, he was preaching each week on Sunday morning, evening, and Wednesday night.

95

Who prayed for him? He did not even know. It really was not important. After all, Jesus is to receive all the glory!

• On special occasions

The Book of 1 Corinthians, Chapter 12, provides insight into special manifestations of the Holy Spirit. These are often referred to as **gifts of the Spirit**. Among this list of nine supernatural gifts are included *faith, healings,* and *miracles.* For ease in remembering these gifts, they are often divided into three categories of three each. Those noted here are defined as *gifts of power.* (The others are *gifts of revelation* and *gifts of utterance.*)

There must be no confusion here. These special manifestations of the Spirit are still effectively operating today.

As part of the New Testament church, each follower of Christ has every right to believe that God has not excluded this generation from the supernatural ministries of the Spirit that were afforded to first century believers.

Surely we need no less of the Spirit today than other times and cultures. Quite likely, as we rapidly approach the end of this age, there is an even greater urgency for the church and individual believers to depend on the power of the Holy Spirit.

Also, the Scripture clearly identifies the Holy Spirit as being in control of these special gifts. *"It is the one and only Holy Spirit who distributes these gifts. He alone decides which gift each person should have"* (1 Corinthians 12:11, NLT). No person can claim ownership of any of these supernatural manifestations of the Spirit. Let me encourage you to carefully study 1 Corinthians 12, 13, 14.

In short, God does use His children on special occasions to minister to specific needs. Be available. Keep your spiritual ears open to the Holy Spirit. You, as a born-again, Spirit-filled believer are a candidate to be the vessel through which the mighty power of God flows. How blessed one is when God imparts a special measure of faith for a special need.

LEVEL FOUR—*SUFFERING FAITH*

Around the world, hundreds of thousands—perhaps even millions—of believers face constant pressure and persecution for their faith in Jesus Christ. The reports are horrific. Everything from family rejection to imprisonment to brutal death is not uncommon in some strong anti-Christian nations. For others, the suffering comes in a much more subtle, nonetheless quite serious, manner. Worship gatherings must be in secret. Witnessing to others is a crime. Social rejection among colleagues and associates, often leading to financial loss, is quite common. As we pray, one of our petitions should be for the persecuted saints who are facing danger every day.

While for the most part the Western world has been spared from such suffering for Christ's sake, there are dark, ominous clouds gathering. From a historical perspective, this nation (USA) has traveled light years away from its moral foundation in the past half century. I do not wish to be a calamity howler; however, as the spirit of antichrist grows, there could be an increased level of persecution.

This should neither come as a surprise nor create fear. Jesus could not have spoken more plainly on this matter. *"When the world hates you, remember it hated me before it hated you. The world would love you if you belonged to it, but you don't. I chose you to come out of the world, and so it hates you"* (John 15:18,19, NLT).

Read the account of Paul's sufferings in 2 Corinthians 11. In his final letter prior to his execution, this champion of faith leaves final instructions to his dear son in the faith, Timothy. Here he solemnly declares his own, now famous, eulogy—*"I have fought a good fight, I have finished my course, I have kept the faith"* (2 Timothy 4:7). However, only a few verses earlier, he speaks of the persecution he has suffered. He concludes, *"Yea, and all that will live godly in Christ Jesus shall suffer persecution"* (2 Timothy 3:12).

The theme of 1 Peter is *suffering for Christ*. Actually, he is encouraging these believers to be victorious in such suffering. Observe how he connects the suffering with rejoicing. *"Beloved, think it not strange concerning the fiery trial which is to try you, as though some strange thing happened to you: But rejoice, inasmuch as ye are partakers of Christ's sufferings; that, when his glory shall be revealed, ye may be* *glad also with <u>exceeding joy</u>"* (1 Peter 4:12,13, NLT, emphasis mine). It is noteworthy that many scholars think his reference to the *fiery trial* was directly associated with Nero who burned live Christians in the palatial gardens to provide light for his immoral orgies.

• Faith that endures

The word *"endure,"* meaning "to persevere," is frequently associated with suffering in Scripture.

"endure hardness, as a good soldier of Jesus Christ" (2 Timothy 2:3).

"endure afflictions..." (2 Timothy 4:5).

Perhaps the most definitive expression of relationship between suffering and faith is found in the book of Hebrews.

"But call to remembrance the former days, in which, after ye were illuminated, ye <u>endured a great fight of afflictions</u>; partly, whilst ye were made a gazingstock both by <u>reproaches and afflictions</u>" (Hebrews 10:32,33, emphasis mine).

Then the author urges these Jewish converts to maintain their faith in the face of suffering. *"Do not throw away this confident trust in the Lord, no matter what happens. Remember the great reward it brings you! Patient endurance is what you need now"* (Hebrews 10:35,36, NLT).

Now we come to Hebrews 11, the *faith chapter* of the New Testament. Eighteen Old Testament characters are identified and each is introduced with the statement, *"by* or *through faith."* Let's select one of them as a reference point. *By faith Moses, when he was come to years, refused to be called the son of Pharaoh's daughter; choosing rather to <u>suffer affliction</u> with the people of God, than to enjoy the pleasures of sin for a season; esteeming the <u>reproach of Christ</u> greater riches than the treasures in Egypt"* (Hebrews 11:24-26, emphasis mine).

In spite of these great testimonies, believers are urged to *"look unto Jesus the author and finisher of our faith; who for the joy that was set before him <u>endured the cross</u>, despising the shame, and is set down at the right hand of the throne of God"* (Hebrews 12:2, emphasis mine).

How does faith endure bitter suffering and persecution? Focus on the outcome. *"If we suffer, we shall also reign with him"* (2 Timothy 2:12). Paul expressed it well. *"For our present troubles are quite small and won't last very long. Yet they produce for us an immeasurably great glory that will last forever! So we don't look at the troubles we can see right now; rather we look forward to what we have not yet seen. For the troubles we see will soon be over, but the joys to come will last forever"* (2 Corinthians 4:17, 18, NLT).

It **really** will be worth it all—when we see Jesus.

LEVEL FIVE—*SUBMISSIVE FAITH*

This is top shelf. It is the combination of all the experiences that have tested or strengthened our faith.

It is the level of faith that without hesitation or reservation, without inner conflict or debilitating fear, without whining or self-pity, simply declares, *"Thy will be done."*

It is a **Job** who can say, *"Though he slay me, yet will I trust in him"* (Job 13:15).

It is an **Esther** who was willing to risk her life to save God's people. *"If I perish, I perish"* (Esther 4:16).

It is a **Paul** on his way to Jerusalem telling the believers gathered at Philip's house in Caesarea, *"What mean ye to weep and to break mine heart? <u>for I am ready not to be bound only, but also to die at Jerusalem for the name of the Lord Jesus</u>"* (Acts 21:13, emphasis mine).

It is the **Lord Jesus Christ** on the way to the cross, praying to His Heavenly Father. *"O my Father, if it be possible, let this cup pass from me: nevertheless not as I will, but as thou wilt"* (Matthew 26:39). Jesus repeated this prayer three times and then faced the farce of a trial, terrible physical torture, and finally the public shame and humiliation of the cross.

It is **millions of unknown saints** who have walked through trials of fire and fought every demonic force of hell and have sung all the way to their eternal home.

"I'm going through, I'm going through,
I'll pay the price whatever others do.
I'll take the way with the Lord's chosen few.
I'm going through, Jesus, I'm going through."

If you are a new follower of Christ, **walk in faith**. If you have been in the Way for many years, **walk in faith**. Wherever you recognize yourself along this pathway, allow your faith to be increased each day. It still has room to grow.

KEEP THE FAITH—JESUS IS COMING SOON!

"The true worshipers are those who worship God in Spirit and in truth. All who believe their prayers will not be heard sin upon the left hand against the scripture in that they go far astray with their unbelief. But those who set times, places, measures, and limits upon God sin upon the right hand and come too close with their tempting of God. So God has forbidden us to err from his commandment on either the left or right, that is, either with unbelief or with tempting. Instead we are to come to God in simple faith, remaining on the straight road, trusting him, and yet setting no bounds.

"Therefore you should confidently expect from God one of two things: either your prayer will be granted, or, that if it is not granted, the granting of it would not be good for you."

—**Martin Luther**

CHAPTER EIGHT

Is Faith *Objective* or *Subjective?*

Our daughter Mischelle's illness was during the very peak of many extreme teachings under the banner of "positive confession." A dear lady who attended the church we were pastoring, and who loved the Lord with all her heart, got caught up in some of these extra-biblical concepts. On one occasion she came to our home to pray for Mischelle, for which we were grateful. However, before praying, she told us that her own grandson had recently been ill and she stomped her feet and commanded the devil to leave the room. Then she emphatically declared, "I pointed my finger toward heaven and said, 'God, if You don't heal my grandson, You are a liar.'"

That's strong language. There are several basic errors with such distortion of scriptural truth.

1. To attempt to *command* God is sheer foolishness.

2. To *question the wisdom* of God is quite arrogant.

3. To *threaten the veracity* of God is more than dangerous.

Quite likely you have heard the old adage: *There is only one God—and you are not Him!*

> **Faith in faith is *result* oriented;**
> **Faith in God is *relationship* oriented.**

• Subjective faith raises questions

If the desired response does not come, then one is left with only two options. 1. God has changed. Of course, any true believer would discount this thought immediately. 2. There is a flaw (weakness) in my faith. Basically this is the only conclusion one can reach. The person paints himself into a corner. It is **my fault** that the answer did not come. There must be sin in my life or, at the very least, a frail, underdeveloped faith.

It should be acknowledged that doubt and unbelief are major deterrents to experiencing divine intervention in human circumstance. Prayer, waiting in the presence of God, learning and assimilating the Word into daily life are vital nourishment to faith building. And, the tendency far too often is to fall back on the sovereignty of God in covering and excusing our lack of faith. In one's heart of hearts each individual is aware of the status of faith in times of crisis.

Let's also look at the other side of this equation. Perhaps I can best do so by again referring to personal experience. When Mischelle was ill, thousands (literally) of believers around the world joined their faith with ours in asking and believing for a healing miracle. Because she did not receive physical healing (here on this earth), undoubtedly someone would counter that no one had mature faith or else she would have been healed. Candidly, I reject such a conclusion. My respect and esteem for the body of Christ rises high above a level that places blame if the answer does not come as I desired.

> **Most doctrinal extremes are an *overemphasis* of a particular biblical truth. In many instances this has developed as the result of an *underemphasis* of that particular truth.**

• Subjective faith is often self-serving

A subjective approach to faith is likely to foster confusion within the family of believers. How? A spiritual elitism develops—a ranking of sorts. Even more tragic is when the primary desires of faith are turned inward. Wealth—material possessions—job promotions—added creature comforts. Such expressions as, "the devil has had the money long enough; it is time for God's people to enjoy it" or "Nothing is too good for the saints" do not measure up to true biblical humility. It is the flesh trying to camouflage itself in spiritual garments. This is Satan's trickery. *The gospel of Christ must work everywhere or it is not valid anywhere.*

Jesus never taught that if you follow Him, you would live in luxury. What He did teach was a life of contentment in the providential care of a loving Heavenly Father.

A major section in the Sermon on the Mount is spent in providing instruction about the proper attitude toward the things of this world. Jesus said it plainly. *"Ye cannot serve both God and money"* (Matthew 7:24, NLT). After telling this group, who were primarily the common working people of His day, not to *"store up treasures here on this earth"* (v. 19) and not to *"worry about everyday life"* or *"having enough food or drink or clothing"* (vv. 25,34), He offers this wonderful assurance. *"Your heavenly Father already knows all your needs, and <u>he will give you all you need</u> from day to day <u>if you live for him</u> and make the <u>Kingdom of God your primary concern</u>"* (Matthew 6:32,33, NLT, emphasis mine).

This is not to vilify those whom God has blessed with material abundance. During our more than 20 years of service at a ministerial training institution, I frequently warned students not to adopt an adversarial position against those who had significant financial resource. In due season they would need to partner with these dedicated followers of Christ to fulfill the vision that God had placed in their hearts.

Our point of reference is not those individuals who have walked in obedience to the commands of the Lord, honored Him with their finances, worked hard, and been good stewards of their blessings. The Bible clearly teaches that if we do these things, His blessings will encompass our lives, both now and for eternity. Rather, the concerns are for those who see "faith" as the means to a better life. For some immature believers who have been exploited by the unscrupulous, it is little more than a substitute for the lottery. Buy a $2 ticket and win millions! God has become synonymous with Santa Claus.

Is this harsh? Listen to the apostle Paul and the apostle Peter not long before each surrendered his earthly life for the cause of Christ.

"These people [false teachers] *always cause trouble. Their minds are corrupt, and they don't tell the truth. To them religion is just a way to get rich. Yet true religion with contentment is great wealth. So if we have enough food and clothing let us be content. For the love of money is the root of all kinds of evil"* (1 Timothy 6:5,6,8,10, NLT, emphasis and explanation mine).

"In their [false teachers] *greed they will make up clever lies to get hold of your money* (2 Peter 2:3,NLT, explanation mine). The King James translation says, *"They with feigned words make merchandise of you."*

• Subjective faith is inconsistent

The lady that I mentioned earlier as demanding that God heal her grandson, died of cancer. In order to uphold her strong position, she attempted to hide her sickness from her own family. Up until about three weeks before she died, they did not even know that she was ill. Her family was devastated.

Now, I do not fault her for choosing to trust God for her healing. Many dear saints have simply believed that God would restore them or take them to heaven. Perhaps there would be more miracles today if true followers of Christ dared to take such a step of faith.

Genuine faith does not attempt to explain away problems or sickness. Genuine faith is never afraid of medical verification. "Not confessing it" makes sickness or problems no less real.

> **Denial of reality is not faith. Looking difficulty square in the eye with confident assurance in the power of the Almighty to change the "reality" is genuine faith.**

This is the inconsistency of subjective faith—faith based on results. While it is scripturally mandated that we publicly express our faith, He is in no way dependent upon our defense of His integrity and power. The simple truth is that we do not have to cover for God. He never changes.

• Faith in God relieves the pressure of outcomes

No, this is not a cop-out. One does not cease to pray and plead with God to intervene in extreme circumstances. Hopefully, we have established that faith must be an integral part of the believer's daily experience. When He intervenes in human experience, there will be supernatural results. To avoid any misunderstanding let it be repeated once more—praying in faith will move the hands of God.

The Scriptures are explicitly clear. Jesus instructed His followers to *"keep on asking"* for answers. Luke tells us, *"One day Jesus told his disciples a story to illustrate their <u>need for constant prayer</u> and to show them that they <u>must never give up</u>"* (Luke 18:1, NLT, emphasis mine).

The parable was about a *"godless judge"* who initially refused to take the case of a desperate widow. I love the language here. *"The judge ignored her for a while, but <u>eventually she wore</u> <u>him out</u>. 'I fear neither God nor man,' he said to himself, 'but this woman is <u>driving me crazy</u>'"* (Luke 18:4,5, NLT, emphasis mine).

Genuine faith is **in** God—the omnipotent, omniscient One—who has both the **power** and the **wisdom** to do whatever is good, right, and best in every circumstance. Why is this such a pivotal issue? Is it mere semantics? I think not.

1. Faith <u>in</u> God provides *assurance* and *peace*, not *confusion* and *distress*.

2. Faith <u>in</u> God eliminates *guilt* if the desired answer does not come when and how I prayed that it would.

3. Faith <u>in</u> God is not only *theologically correct,* it also becomes a powerful tool for *witnessing to unbelievers*.

4. Faith <u>in</u> God bespeaks of a *relationship of unrestricted trust* in His *love, mercy,* and *grace*.

It is this dimension of maturing faith—*level five faith*—that looks into the face of *distress, disaster, disease*, or even *death* and finds an inner peace that cannot be manufactured or sustained by human will or endeavor.

• Objective faith is not emotionally controlled

All of us have emotions, and by personality mix some allow their emotions to be openly expressed more frequently than others. Depending on your persuasion, that may or may not be viewed as healthy or helpful. However, I rather suspect that all of us soon grow weary with the person whose whole approach to life is emotionally controlled. Perhaps you have already had a name scamper through your mind and gave a big sigh or rolled your eyes back at the mere thought.

From time to time the child of God may encounter sudden, dramatic circumstances that are worse than being hit in the stomach by a heavyweight fighter. Do emotions soar? Absolutely. And, there is nothing wrong with that and nothing to be ashamed of. Now enters the faith factor. Those frazzled emotions are soothed by heaven's balm and a calm serenity blossoms forth. Realistically, this may not be a 30 minute treatment and instantaneously everything is back to normal. At times the battle is long and difficult, no light appears at the end of the tunnel. Yet, it is wondrous to have a firm grip on the gentle hand of God as He leads you through the maze of anxiety and pain. Fear and confusion melt like snow on a warm spring day. God is in control.

> **Mountaintop "feelings" are wonderful, but deep valley faith guides us through the darkness to triumph.**

The person whose spiritual life is consistently dependent on peak-level emotion will seldom experience the peaceful security of absolute confidence that is the hallmark of mature faith. A line from an old song says it well: *"I can feel His hand in mine, that's all I need to know."*

• What is the lesson in this ordeal?

From the Book of Job we learn that at times God allows Satan to take his best shot at a believer. God's assessment of Job is spoken like a proud father.

"Then the Lord asked Satan, 'Have you noticed my servant Job? He is the finest man in all the earth—a man of complete integrity. He fears God and will have nothing to do with evil'" (Job 1:8, NLT). Of course Satan countered by saying that Job was serving God for selfish purposes. Whereupon God gave Satan permission to attack Job. *"All right, you may test him. Do whatever you want, with everything he possesses, but don't harm him physically"* (Job 1:12, NLT).

When Job had aced this test, God again bragged to Satan about him. This time God added, *"And he has maintained his integrity, even though you persuaded me to harm him without cause"* (Job 2:3, NLT). Here the devil ups the ante. *"Take away his health, and he will surely curse you to your face!"* (Job 2:5, NLT). And, God allowed Job to be tested further. In his emaciated condition, Job struggled. Who wouldn't? But, he never lost faith and in the end was victorious.

The natural mind judges that to be unfair. But, mature faith sees a whole different scenario. God was saying to Satan,

"I can trust my servant Job, because he trusts Me." Have you ever wondered if God has said the same to Satan about you? Is your faith at that level of maturity? None of us are anxious to pick a fight of this sort with the devil. However, if it comes, and our faith is in God, not in the immediate, visible results, the ultimate outcome can only be victory.

Thankfully, most of the trials of life are not so dramatic as those recorded in the account of Job. So, we must look from a more pragmatic view. <u>What lesson do I need to learn</u> that will enhance my spiritual growth and development? What is God saying to me through this experience?

The contemporary chorus, *Refiner's Fire,* employs Old Testament language relating to the purification process of gold and silver. It is in the heat that the impurities are separated from gold and silver. The *refiner's fire* in not intended to destroy, but by this process increase the worth of the gold or silver. Likewise, trials test the spiritual metal (faith) of the believer (see Isaiah 48:10; Zechariah 13:9; Malachi 3:2,3).

> *One of the ongoing lessons that God is attempting to teach us is to be separated from worldlike attitudes and actions. And, it may well take the fire for us to see impurities that have mingled into the mix of our daily lives.*

Another distinctive purpose of God is for His children to develop in His own likeness. (Remember *Sanctifying Faith*—set apart from and set apart unto.) In the early verses of 2 Corinthians, Paul addresses this divine reasoning. *"He [God the Father] is the source of every mercy and the God who comforts us. <u>He comforts us in all our troubles so that we can comfort others.</u> When others are troubled, we will be able to give them the same comfort God has given us. For when God comforts us, it is so that we, in turn, can be an encouragement to you"* (2 Corinthians 1:3,4,6, NLT, emphasis and explanation mine).

> **The battle scars that you wear can be a powerful means to** *empathetically* **and** *sympathetically* **encourage others to never give up or doubt the veracity of God's promises.**

God never intends to push any of His children away from Him. He does not have favorites. His love for one is not greater that His love for another. Rather, His desire is to draw each of us into a closer fellowship that will radiate His nature to others. Mature faith comprehends this truth.

James had an unusual first few lines in his letter. If you need to capture your audience with a beginning statement, I suspect that he did so. Listen. *"Dear brothers and sisters, <u>whenever trouble comes your way, let it be an opportunity for joy.</u> For when your faith is tested, your endurance has a chance to grow. So let it grow, for when your endurance is fully developed, you will be strong in character and ready for anything"* (James 1:2-4, NLT, emphasis mine).

The apostle Paul added a similar word in the book of Romans following the remarkable defense of *justification by faith* and the hope it brings. *"We can rejoice, too, when we run into <u>problems and trials</u>, for we know that <u>they are good for us</u>—they help us learn to endure. And endurance develops strength of character in us, and character strengthens our confident expectation of salvation"*(Romans 5:3,4, NLT, emphasis mine).

Trials will lead you to a new dimension of *tender compassion* or they will drive you to a place of *bitter resentment*. The choice is yours.

The reaction we have to difficulties and extreme crisis situations will, to a large degree, fashion the positive or negative impact these adversities have on our lives. The Scriptures do not teach that we can "confess" away the undesirable events that come in this depraved, sin-dominated world. But, they certainly give no occasion for whining and self-pity that belittle the power and wisdom of the sovereign Lord of the ages. If you have mature faith—you will discover the hand of God on every page of your life's record. And, in due time when you reread each chapter, you will discern that He is always a *good, gracious, compassionate, caring, loving* Father.

As a boy, I loved to listen to the stories of God's faithfulness during the earlier, very difficult days in our nation. Those old veterans of the faith spoke with tender voice and moist eyes as they told (often repeating the same stories) of how God has "seen them through." My own life was shaped by such stalwart saints. Now, I find myself asking the Lord to help me become a person who, by *past experience* and *present example,* can speak words of faith and encouragement to those younger in their walk with the Lord. From my perspective, it is a high and noble goal to show others that our faith is <u>in</u> God.

CHAPTER NINE

Learning to Trust

The humorous story is told of the man who fell off a cliff in the night and on the way down he grabbed onto the scrawny limb of a small tree growing out of the rocks. Hanging there tenaciously, he cried loudly, "O God, please help me." A voice from heaven came booming back, "Turn loose of the limb." He called out again for God to help him. Again, the same response, "Turn loose of the limb." In desperation he shouted, "Is there anyone else up there who can help me?"

> The *walk of faith* never evolves into a walk of sight.
> *Trust* in the Lord is absolutely essential to a vibrant,
> healthy spiritual life.

The title of this chapter is chosen carefully. *Learning to trust* is a lifelong process. Suddenly, one day you will not discover that it is a done deal—now I know how to trust God. Often I have found that just about the time I begin to think that I understand this whole concept, there is something of a different dimension that comes creeping or bursting onto the scene. The old song, *'Tis So Sweet To Trust in Jesus* is a favorite for many saints. However, I find myself slightly modifying the last verse, "*I'm so glad I've <u>learned to trust Him</u>*" to say, "*I'm so glad I'm <u>learning to trust Him</u>.*"

The fact is, God planned it this way. Human nature tends to be proud and independent. However, it is not only the initial salvation experience that requires faith. That is basic **level one faith**. It is faith in the finished work of the Cross that restores the relationship with God that had been shattered by sin. Every born-again believer understands that there is no other way to eternal life. But, this is just the beginning.

The craving to *be in control* lurks in the shadows like a nocturnal animal of prey ready to pounce at a moment's notice. Allowing God full access and governance of every aspect of life is indeed a challenge. Are there problem areas? Of course. But some things we can handle ourselves. We are comfortably confident of personal abilities. The fishermen turned disciples thought they could handle a boat on the Sea of Galilee—until the storm came.

Growing up I was taught that life does not owe you anything except an opportunity. If there are adversities and reverses you don't whine and complain. Life can be tough. There are injustices—but never sit in the corner and suck your thumb, feeling sorry for yourself. So, as a young man my resolve was strong. Somewhat of a Christianized version of you control your own destiny. But, there came the day when a particular situation was overpowering to my emotions. I sat in the floor and admitted, "I can't handle this anymore." This was not classroom theory. This was eyeball to eyeball with reality. As painful as those days were, it was a valuable learning experience. I had to trust God. And, it worked.

It is much easier to be objective about the path that another may be walking. How often have we glibly said or someone has said to us, "Just trust God, He will take care of everything." It is certainly true, but stretches our faith to release the outcome to His infinite wisdom.

I saw a postcard that read, "When you are in the middle of a marsh filled with alligators, it is often difficult to remember that you are there to drain the swamp." However, it is at these nowhere-to-go dead-end alleys that His presence can be *calming, reassuring*, and *strengthening*.

"Casting the whole of your care—all your <u>anxieties</u>, all your <u>worries</u>, all your <u>concerns</u>, <u>once and for all</u>—on Him; for He <u>cares for you</u> affectionately, and <u>cares about you</u> watchfully" (1 Peter 5:7, Amp., emphasis mine).

We rejoice in the faith and trust of Bible characters who in times of grave danger experienced such marvelous victories. Remember, however, they did not know the outcome. They were living through the situation moment by moment. This is what real trust is all about. When the night is midnight black and there is no moon or stars above and you have no clue which direction to take, do you panic? Do you bolt and run? No, as a mature child of God, you hold to His unchanging hand and patiently wait for the dawn to come. He will be there with you and for you.

The words *trust, trusted, trustest* are used approximately 180 times in Scripture. Almost 70 of those expressions are found in the Book of Psalms. In these inspiring songs, which give verbal articulation to the whole gamut of man's feelings and emotions, there is frequent reference both specifically and directly to *"trusting in the Lord."*

David penned it so beautifully when he had been taken captive by the Philistines in Gath. *"But when I am afraid, I put my trust in you"* (Psalm 56:3, NLT, emphasis mine). He did not say "if" I am afraid, but "when" I am afraid. Here is the dynamic conclusion he reaches in this song. *"This I know: God is on my side. O God, I praise your word. Yes, Lord, I praise your word. I trust in God, so why should I be afraid?"* (Psalm 56:9-11, NLT, emphasis mine).

• All things—not just one

"What benefit could possibly come from this?" is a frequent question, even within the fellowship of believers. More likely than not the reference is to one single incident. At times we must remind ourselves that one small piece does not reveal the whole picture of the puzzle. There are some odd-shaped and strange-colored pieces that do not seem to *fit* anywhere. Only in the light of eternity will the revelation be complete.

It may be an oversimplification of a profound truth, but Romans 8:28 clearly says *"all things work together for good."* This is not a pick-and-choose game. Two good—three bad. No, the Scripture says **all**. Notice, however, that this is a restricted promise. It refers to those who *"love God"* and *"have been called according to his purpose."*

> **God is never surprised or confused by what is transpiring at any given millisecond in your life. He has not retreated to the back room trying to come up with Plan B because Plan A just failed.**

Again, the significance of trust quickly surfaces. Since *all things* are not always pleasant and comfortable (refer to Romans 8:35-39), it is imperative that we counter the natural tendency to *distress, discouragement,* and *defeat* with confidence in the Almighty. He knows the end from the beginning and all points between. I see only the present, which at times may be rather foggy. He has an eternal purpose and every marker along the way is for my good. What a wonderful God we serve. *He deserves to be trusted.*

• This time it's different

In Chapters 1 and 2, I attempted to recount two totally different ways in which God intervened in difficult human circumstances. In this journey of learning to trust, it is almost certain that there will be a rather extensive accumulation and broad spectrum of tests along the way. Two axioms seem to be self-evident at this point.

1. There are no fixed patterns to the problems of life.

Having been in higher education for a number of years, I often found it quite amusing to hear students discuss professors and the types of tests they gave. There were the "true-false" professors, the "multiple choice," the "objective," and, of course, the dreaded "essay" professors. The sharp students soon learned how and what to study in preparing for the various tests. But, horror of horrors were those totally uncompassionate profs who never prepared the same style test twice. They were so disconcerting that the students had to really study for their tests.

Sometimes I think we are not unlike those collegians who wanted to earn grades with the minimum effort. But God is too smart for that. In His unlimited knowledge and infinite wisdom, He prepares the appropriate test for each individual. How delighted the Heavenly Father must be when one of His choice children aces the test—by trusting in Him.

2. There are no standardized formulas for resolving problems.

Have you ever wondered why Jesus employed a variety of methods in healing the sick? Some He touched; others He simply spoke the word. But there were other occasions in which He used spit and dirt. He told some to *"rise up and walk"* and said to others, *"go and sin no more"* or *"go show yourself to the priest."* Why? In my opinion to (a) show that God's power is uniquely unlimited and (b) to keep foolish man from attempting to emulate and depend on a specific method.

He fed a hungry crowd who had listened to Him preach all day. He spoke the word from a boat to calm a storm, but also walked on the turbulent water to His disciples on that same sea. He turned water (probably not pure) into the best wine of the marriage feast. On the other hand, He took a whip and drove the moneychangers and sellers of animals out of the Temple.

It is such a tremendous blessing and faith-building encouragement to witness God at work in His own unique manner. Have you ever been surprised and amazed at God's way? His plan may not (probably will not) be accomplished in the logical procedure man would *assume, expect,* or *attempt*—but His way is always *right, good,* and *best*!

> *"Trust in the Lord with all your heart; do not depend on your own understanding. Seek his will in all you do, and he will direct your paths"* (Proverbs 3:5,6, NLT).

• What about him?

Human comparisons are dangerous and faith destroying. There will always be those who seem to be more in tune with God than you; there will always be those who seem to be less in tune with God than you. If you compare yourself with the former, it will bring discouragement. If you compare yourself with the latter, it will bring pride. This is almost a universal temptation among believers, as the carnal nature loves recognition and preeminence.

> **To put another person down in order to elevate yourself is grossly sinful. At the very least it is an expression of the lack of trust in God who is ordering the steps of your life.**

Paul warns and instructs the Corinthians concerning this matter of comparison. Incidentally, the Greek word he uses for *"compare"* bears the connotation of evaluation or judging. That is, setting a standard. Naturally, the comparison would be in our favor. Listen to the inspired Word.

> *"Oh, don't worry; I wouldn't dare say that I am as wonderful as these other men who tell you how important they are! But they are only <u>comparing themselves with each other</u>, and <u>measuring themselves by themselves</u>. What foolishness!"* (2 Corinthians 10:12, NLT, emphasis mine).

> *"As the Scriptures say, 'The person who wishes to boast should boast only of what the Lord has done.' When people boast about themselves, it doesn't count for much. But when the Lord commends someone, that's different!"* (2 Corinthians 10:17,18, NLT).

Following the resurrection of Christ, the disciples returned to Galilee. Peter, and six other disciples, had gone back to his former place of security—fishing boat and nets. According to John's record (John 21), they had fished all night and caught absolutely nothing. In circumstances similar to the first call of Simon to leave his fishing nets to become a *"fisher of men,"* Jesus again challenged Peter, *"Follow me."*

In the conversation that ensued between Jesus and Peter, John was eavesdropping. I love this guy—he always wanted to be in on what Jesus was doing. In his peripheral vision Peter saw John standing there, and asked, *"What about him, Lord?"*

The answer of Christ seems rather blunt. *"If I want him to remain alive until I return, <u>what is that to you</u>? You follow me"* (John 21:21,22, NLT, emphasis mine). Peter, it is none of your business! Do you suppose that the Lord needs to say that to some of His children today? "Stop being concerned about what others are or are not doing and keep you eyes on Me."

Now, let's illustrate from Scripture why simple trust is always the appropriate response. Again, this narrative involves the apostle Peter. This event is after the ascension of Christ and outpouring of the Holy Spirit at Pentecost. Peter, James, and John (often called the inner circle of Jesus) had assumed leadership roles in the infant Church located in Jerusalem.

King Herod Agrippa had James killed with a sword (Acts 12:1). When he saw how much this pleased the Jewish religious leaders, he arrested Peter intending to bring him to public trial. Herod must have suspected something—he ordered 16 soldiers to guard Peter and put him in the inner prison during the Passover celebration.

The night before Peter was to be brought to trial, he was asleep, chained between two of the guards. I find this rather amazing. Such trust in God that he was sleeping, knowing that his fate could be the same as James' within a few hours. The account of his miraculous deliverance is thrilling. The details are found in Acts 12.

While Peter was in prison, *"the church prayed very earnestly for him"* (Acts 12:5, NLT). On the eve of his trial, *"many were gathered for prayer"* (Acts 12:12, NLT) at the home of Mary, the mother of John Mark. God answered their prayers. He changed an impossible circumstance.

However, it would be my conclusion that these same people were praying with the same fervency and yet James was put to death, not delivered like Simon Peter. Why did this happen? One killed and the other delivered. Does God have favorites? Certainly not. Could God have delivered James in the same miraculous manner that He delivered Peter? Of course He could. It boils down to trusting in the sovereign God.

It is here that many believers have deep struggles with their faith. Digging below the surface emotions, you will frequently discover that the issue is one of *comparisons.* "I love God as much as Sister XYZ. I prayed. I have faith," with the implication being that the maturity of my faith was as much or more than others.

One of Satan's most insidious lies is to attempt to convince believers that God loves others more than He loves them. Surely, IF God really cared, He would never allow such horrible things to happen. Don't be deceived. God's love is not measured on a scale of 1 – 10. He loves you equally—no more, no less—with all His moral creation.

• How Can I Reach this Level of Trust

1. Remember that this is a *lifelong learning process.* Every challenging event of life is intended by God to draw you closer to Him. Never does He desire to push you away.

2. Maintain a close relationship with the Lord *before you face the crisis.* It is unwise to put God on the shelf until there is an emergency and then run to Him for help. Your <u>daily devotional</u> time is absolutely critical to a healthy spiritual life. Attend God's house regularly.

3. Attach yourself to some *mature saints* who have been walking this Way for many years. Ask them to become your prayer partners. Listen to their testimonials of supernatural intervention. Listen even more carefully to their stories of walking through deep valleys by the grace of God. Observe the tender heart and compassionate spirit they possess.

4. Learn to *control your emotions.* Don't make rash, foolish statements. Don't automatically jump to the worst possible conclusions. Allow your spirit time to filter through the various components of the situation before you make a resolute decision.

5. Look to the *Word of God* as your first source book for the appropriate actions and reactions. Remember, ***the Word presents the <u>principles</u>; the Holy Spirit applies the <u>particulars</u>.*** It is the only truly reliable source of guidance.

6. *Subjugate your will to the will of God quickly.* In simple terms, recognize that God is sovereign. One of the certain evidences of trust in the Almighty is to be able to

joyfully surrender to the eternal dimension that He has begun to work in and through you here on this earth.

7. View the *events of this life as very temporary*. Life at its longest is quite brief when placed alongside the eternal future. Paul encourages us. *"For our present troubles are quite small and won't last very long. Yet they produce for us an immeasurably great glory that will last forever! So we don't look at the troubles we can see right now; rather, we look forward to what we have not yet seen. For the troubles we see will soon be over, but the joys to come will last forever"* (2 Corinthians 4:17,18, NLT, emphasis mine).

CHAPTER TEN

Your *Personalized* Life

There is only one YOU. You are so unique that no one else in all the universe can be mistaken for you. In doing research recently, I found some amazing information pertaining to the creative genius of God. The genetic material that determines a person's inherited features (sex, blood type, eye color, etc.) is called **DNA** (deoxyribonucleic acid). DNA is a long molecule that is made up of building blocks called *nucleotides*. These nucleotides are grouped together to form the genes. Each person's DNA contains over 40,000 genes. One or more genes determine each inherited feature. The arrangement of the nucleotides in the DNA is extremely significant. *Every person's order of nucleotides in the DNA is unique.* A statement such as this, verified by the most astute medical minds, should dramatically increase our reverence for the awesome God we serve.

Very quickly this thought progression leads one to

being overwhelmed by how much God must love each of us. He did not create clones. No two people who have ever lived are exactly alike, from fingerprints to personality to physical features. There is no debate on this subject. Consequently, it is not a stretch of faith (or logic) to conclude that He has a *unique* master plan for each *unique* person. If we follow the plan He has ordained for us, it will produce a life of *joy, peace*, and *contentment* in the security of His love and grace.

One need only consider men and women of biblical record to observe how God provides opportunity to individually become a participant in His redemptive relationship with humanity. However, before we proceed in this discussion, it is imperative to remember the Triune God's bottom-line purpose for man. Peter reminds us that God *"is long suffering to us-ward, <u>not willing that any should perish</u>, but that all should come to repentance"* (2 Peter 3:9, emphasis mine). So, the very first step for any person to qualify in this eternal enterprise is *by faith* to accept Jesus Christ as both <u>*Savior*</u> and <u>*Lord*</u>. This is not redundant. Many have been disappointed by the presumed absence of divine guidance, when in fact they have chosen a road with barricades marked "Do Not Enter."

The full promise of God's blessings comes within the framework of obedience. There are two words that a believer can never say. They are *No, Lord*. For when you say *no*, He is no longer your *Lord*.

Abraham was chosen by God to be the *father of the faithful*. Through him, all the nations of the world would be blessed. The covenant promises God made with Abraham were literal and will be completely and specifically fulfilled during the millennial reign of Christ.

Moses, whose life was miraculously spared, received training both in the palace and in the wilderness to become the chosen *administrative* and *spiritual* leader to escort the Children of Israel out of Egyptian slavery. One cannot read the account of this man without noting the direct correlation between his life and the blueprint God had drawn for His chosen people.

David, the shepherd, songwriter, second king of Israel, was a *man after God's own heart* from whose family the Savior of the world, Jesus Christ, was to be born. The promise of God was that there would be a ruler on *his throne forever.*

Mary, the young, unknown Jewish peasant girl, submitted to the plan of God and miraculously conceived our Savior. It is next to impossible to comprehend the emotional trauma this must have created for this sincere, pure follower of the Law of Moses. This had never happened before, ever. Talk about faith!

Paul, the Jewish religious leader who became a devout follower of Jesus, expended his life carrying the message of *salvation by faith in Christ alone* to the Jews, Gentiles, and world rulers. His contribution to the Church lives on today through the 13 books of the New Testament he wrote.

By now most of us are saying, "Yes, but those were Bible characters. I certainly do not fit into that category." True, not everyone is going to be granted such notoriety in fulfilling his or her spiritual commission. But, God has a good word for the likes of us.

Think about this—there is no one else who has been chosen to do exactly what He is asking you to do. God thinks you are just as valuable as the person who preaches to thousands. *It is not a matter of worth—it is simply a matter of assignment.* **Your contribution to the Kingdom is of inestimable worth.**

"Remember, dear brothers and sisters, that few of you were wise in the world's eyes, or powerful, or wealthy when God *called you. Instead, God deliberately chose things the world considers foolish in order to shame those who think they are wise. And he chose those that are powerless to shame those that are powerful. God chose things despised by the world, things counted as nothing at all, and used them to bring to nothing what the world considers impor- tant, so that no one can ever boast in the presence of God"* (1 Corinthians 1:26-29, NLT, emphasis mine).

Later in this first letter to the Corinthian church, Paul elaborates on the importance of each member in the body of Christ. *"The human body has many parts, but the many parts make up only one body. So it is with the body of Christ. But God made our bodies with many parts, and he* *has put each part just where he wants it. What a strange thing a body would be if it had only one part. <u>Now all of you together are Christ's body, and each of you is a separate and necessary part of it</u>"* (1 Corinthians 12: 12,18-19,27, NLT, emphasis mine).

• Connecting the dots

Do you recall drawing pictures by connecting the dots? Somewhere along the way the picture began to come into focus. Finally, you were racing toward the last dot to complete the picture. A life of faith is like that. As you move to each prescribed "dot" that God has placed in developing the picture of your life, the purpose begins to become meaningful.

I was called to preach in a junior Sunday School class at age nine. It was a dramatic moment in my young life. But, I certainly did not have a clue what would be involved and how God would order the days ahead. At age 17, I began preaching on a fairly consistent basis. Still, as sincere as I was, my mind did not give birth to the faintest notion of where this was heading.

Now, looking back down a winding trail of more than four decades, I stand in utter amazement at the pathway the Lord had prepared. It has been far beyond the scope of my wildest imagination. *"O Lord, you are my God; I will exalt you and praise your name, for in <u>perfect faithfulness</u> you have done marvelous things, <u>things planned long ago</u>"* (Isaiah 25:1, NIV, emphasis mine).

Have there been struggles? Of course. Disappointments? Some of major proportion. Have there been victories? More than I can possibly enumerate. Would I trade my "dots" for another set? Not in a million years!

Allow me to digress for a moment. On more than one occasion I have spoken with a person who has serious reservations about following the plan of God for his or her life. For some reason—perhaps from the negative comments they have heard or the sour attitudes they have been subjected to—this individual has come to the erroneous conclusion that a life of obedience is dull and boring, or worse yet, like a big dose of horrible tasting medicine. In order to please God, you must be totally miserable. Don't ever buy into such nonsense.

The most satisfying place that any of us can ever hope to find on this earth is right in the very center of God's purpose and will. However, this fulfillment must not be confused with easy or comfortable. Problems, or the lack thereof, do not and cannot define God's unique plan for your life.

Again, this is a point at which there is often confusion. If this is God's will for my life, then why is it so difficult? Really such a question should not tantalize the mind of a believer. Go into the locker room of a football team that has just won the Super Bowl. Are they sitting around grousing about how painful it was or counting the number of times they got knocked down or stepped on? That may be a rather poor analogy, but we can always turn to our Lord as an example of commitment that we would do well to emulate.

Jesus left His place at the Father's right hand and condescended to become a human that He might fulfill a specific mission. At His baptism by John the Baptist in the river of Jordan, Jesus had full comprehension of why He was here on earth. In the symbolism of death, burial, and resurrection, Christ set forth on His public ministry with the *visible approval* of the Holy Spirit (sat on Him in the form of a dove) and the *verbal approval* of the Father (*"This is my beloved Son, in whom I am well pleased"*).

During the next three years, Jesus often explained how He measured other things in the light of doing His Father's will.

"My nourishment comes from doing the will of God, who sent me, and from finishing his work" (John 4:34, NLT).

"For even I, the Son of Man, came here not to be served but to serve others, and to give my life as a ransom for many" (Mark 10:45, NLT, emphasis mine).

Hours before the crucifixion, He confided in the disciples, *"Now my soul is deeply troubled. Should I pray, 'Father, save me from what lies ahead'? But that is the very reason why I came! Father, bring glory to your name"* (John 12:27,28, NLT, emphasis mine).

The writer of Hebrews arduously reminds these Jewish believers of the *faith* of Old Testament saints (Chapter 11). Also, he strongly admonishes them to comprehend the unwavering *faith that Christ displayed* in fulfilling His earthly mission as the basis for holding firmly to their faith.

"And let us <u>run with endurance the race that God has set before us</u>. We do this by keeping our eyes on Jesus, on whom our faith depends from start to finish.* <u>He was willing to die a shameful death on the cross because of the joy he knew would be his afterward</u>. Now he is seated in the place of highest honor beside God's throne in heaven. Think about all he endured when sinful people did such terrible things to him, <u>so that you don't become weary and give up</u>" (Hebrews 12:1-3, NLT, emphasis mine). (*Also translated as the Originator and Perfecter of our faith.)

• **Step by step**

Joseph, of Old Testament fame, is often cited as a type of Christ in that there is no evil spoken of him in Scripture. Ultimately, as the prime minister in Egypt, he saved the then known world from famine and starvation. But it surely did not start out that way for him. As the favorite son of his father Israel (Jacob), his 10 half brothers hated him with a passion. That animosity peaked when one evening at the dinner table he boldly announced that someday they would all bow down before him. Talk about sibling rivalry! It was true, but certainly not destined to happen at breakfast the next morning. This was to be an extended process that required a high concentration of faith. Joseph had to *really believe* that his life was in the protective care of God's hand.

The first step for young Joseph (he was 17) was the **pit.** From here he was sold to traveling merchants and was taken into Egypt to be auctioned on the slave block. Once in Egypt, a high ranking official named Potiphar purchased him. Soon temptation came to this handsome young man as Potiphar's wife tried repeatedly to seduce him. Joseph was thrown into **prison**—for refusing to be immoral. Ultimately, by a series of divinely orchestrated events, he moved into the **palace.** Now he is 30 years of age, but it is nine more years before he sees his brothers again. It was 22 years from the time he announced God's plan until it actually became a reality. (To discover all the intriguing details of this Old Testament narrative read Genesis 29-45.)

Joseph was a person of integrity and served faithfully in Potiphar's house and in prison. How easily he could have reasoned, "God has forsaken me or I wouldn't be here in Egypt as a slave or a prisoner." It would be superfluous to guess at the struggles that went on in his mind: was the vision really from God? Will I ever see my father again. Did I do anything to deserve this? On and on a list could go. How he handled the pressure is not known. Even in success, Joseph did not succumb to the temptation to rely on his own abilities. What we do know for certain is that he did not lose his faith.

What you do today has an irreversible impact on tomorrow. Your decisions today become granite monuments to future happiness or remorseful memorials to future heartaches.

• Overcome or Overcompensate—it's up to you

Make no mistake about it I do not sit with the extremists who deny reality. Life can be bitter at times. There are problems in our world, vomited out from satanic control of depraved man. Even the most godly saints feel the pain that is the inevitable consequence of rebellion and disobedience.

Nor can I agree with those who believe that you simply repeat a scriptural mantra and eventually you will have exactly what you want. Unfortunately, some of what has been promoted under the banner of faith ministry has been a camouflaged appeal to man's hedonistic nature. Far too many have had their faith shipwrecked while trying to accommodate fleshly desires. *The longing of true faith is to humbly submit as a willing servant to the Most High God.* However, on the other hand, there are those who proudly embrace the hard things of life. It has become a point of identification for them—a way to get attention. Honestly, there are individuals who would not have anything to talk about if they were not living right on the edge of the next disaster.

Neither of these positions are exemplary of true faith. Biblical faith penetrates our spirit. This will preclude a grasping for personal gratification and self-centered expectations. The Spirit within will also bring our emotions into a proper balance in times of anxiety and distress.

The human spirit that is *guarded* and *guided* by the Holy Spirit will experience a godly contentment.

Perhaps part of the problem lies in our longing to be vindicated. To show that we have faith, we want God to do something—right now—and make bold pronouncements about *what, when, where,* and *how* He is going to respond. In some ways being on the offensive is quite legitimate as we battle against the devil. We delight in being able to give him a swift kick in the seat of the pants.

However, the area of concern surfaces in attempting to maintain a good image among our believing friends or to save face with unbelievers who know our faith walk. If **the** answer does not arrive in a timely fashion, *submissive faith* (Level Five Faith) does not become angry or discouraged.

Trusting God relieves the *pressure of performance* and replaces it with the *serenity of assurance*.

Here are a few suggestions on how to have overcoming faith through the various seasons and dimensions of life.

1. Realize that God has arranged a unique, personal plan for your life. You do not have to compete with anyone else, nor should you ever attempt to do so.

2. Refuse to make comparisons. Your loving Heavenly Father created you to honor and worship Him. Your place in His *family* is not in some ranking system. The experiences of others do not determine His plan for your life. If you love and obediently serve Him, then He will be pleased.

3. Never accuse God of treating you unfairly in the various circumstances of life you encounter. He is fully aware at all times of each event of your life. *He always knows what is best.*

4. Through the Word and prayer maintain a daily relationship with the Lord. Believe that the Word is *inspired, infallible Truth.* Believe that God *hears* and *answers prayer.* When difficulty comes, you will be armed with the *"sword of the Spirit"* (Word of God) and the *"shield of faith"* to withstand enemy aggression.

5. Publicly express your faith in God. Never be ashamed or hesitant to speak to others about your personal faith. This will strengthen you in your Christian walk.

6. Avoid extreme teachings that emphasize faith as the entryway to secure wealth and material possessions. Do not evaluate the level of your faith by your earthly *possessions, position* or *prestige.*

7. Place your confident trust in the Lord during times of crisis. Remember that mature faith is in God—not in the results. *His way is always the right way.*

8. Keep hope for the eternal home alive in your heart. This life is temporary; we are simply passing through. God is faithful—heaven is real—Jesus is coming very soon!

Epilogue

Trying to codify your faith development is almost as futile as trying to watch a child grow. But, as you *faithfully* follow the Lord in obedience, it does happen. The mom who buys school clothes from year to year suddenly realizes that her little one is not so small anymore. For the believer, the situation that may have seemed to loom larger than Mount Everest in past years is nothing more than a back yard molehill today.

> *Take courage.*
> *God has not changed—but your faith is changing you.*

Still have questions? Certainly. Will any of us ever reach a place of perfection in our faith? Not likely. In my opinion, the apostle Thomas, whose name is frequently associated with the uncomplimentary term, *doubting*, had a growing faith. Finally, after the resurrection, he proclaimed *"My Lord and my God!"* (John 20:28).

God is never angered by the sincere questions of a searching believer. He is far more displeased with the fake faith of one who has never experienced the reality of relationship.

Hopefully, as you read this volume, you have reached a new level of appreciation for some basic truths.

1. God is a delightfully personal God. He is all powerful, but also all knowing/wise. Man was created at His initiative, not because He "needed" approval or acceptance to be complete, rather so that his moral creation could participate in the fellowship of His eternal perfection.

2. God's plan for man's redemption is only received by faith. So, from the beginning, the relationship that He unilaterally offered to depraved mankind was founded in faith. This is vitally important to the concept of a living faith.

3. The development of faith is a lifelong process. From one pole of the variegated spectrum of life's events to the other, faith is required to meet the challenge. While there are no clear lines of demarcation from one step to the next, there are clearly defined aspects of faith in Scripture.

a. Saving Faith
b. Sanctifying Faith
c. Supernatural Faith
d. Suffering Faith
e. Submissive Faith

From careful study of God's Word and years of attempting to walk according to its principles, I am convinced that *submissive faith* is the highest level of faith. It in no way undermines or negates the whole principle or any aspect of faith. Rather, the opposite is true. *Submissive faith* brings a cohesive unity to all that we *believe, are,* and *do.*

4. Trusting God in every circumstance, while serving Him in obedience, provides genuine joy, peace, and fulfillment in life. Paul never wanted anyone to feel sorry for him. He gladly *"discarded everything else, counting it all as garbage, so that I may have Christ and become one with him"* (Philippians 3:8, NLT). The words of an old song express it quite well. "The longer I serve Him, the sweeter He grows. The more that I love Him, more love He bestows. Each day is like heaven, my heart overflows, the longer I serve Him, the sweeter He grows."

Please be encouraged in your faith. Guard it carefully. It is your key to abundant life now and eternal life in the future.

If you have been disappointed in others or in yourself, resolve that issue at the Cross. Keep looking to Jesus.

If you are in the middle of the biggest firestorm you have ever faced, remember the battle is not yours—it is the Lord's. He has never been defeated, in spite of what may appear to be at the moment.

> *Marry your faith to God's sovereignty.*
> *It is a marriage that was planned in heaven,*
> *made for earth, and will last for all eternity.*

KEEP THE FAITH!

143

ADDITIONAL BOOKS
by

H. Maurice Lednicky

FADED GLORY: The Church in a Cultural Crisis

The Scriptures Applied, Volume I

The Scriptures Applied, Volume II

The Scriptures Applied, Volume III

Insights from the Word: A Collection of Scriptural Truth

ORDER FROM

LIFESTYLE MINISTRIES
1431 EAST BURNTWOOD
SPRINGFIELD, MISSOURI 65803

Email: **mmlednicky@aol.com**

Website: **mmlednicky-lifestyleministries.org**